Sc. .... Deliverance I

Receive and Maintain Your Deliverance

On Legal Grounds

by

Dr. Pauline Walley

Foreword by Rev. Greg Mauro

SCHOOL OF DELIVERANCE I
Receive and Maintain Your Deliverance On Legal Grounds

Dr. Pauline Walley

Copyright © 1997 Pauline Walley
Copyright © 2002 Pauline Walley
Copyright © 2005 Pauline Walley

First Publication, London, UK, 1996
Second Publication, New York, USA, 2005

Copyright © 2005 by Dr. Pauline Walley

Printed in the United States of America

ISBN 1-59781-777-5

Unless otherwise indicated, Scripture references are from the New King James version of the Bible. Copyright © 1990, 1985, 1983 by Thomas Nelson, Inc.

www.xulonpress.com

Dedication

This book is dedicated to the Almighty God, the Creator of mankind, who sent me to this world to minister healing and deliverance unto the captive and the broken-hearted. I acknowledge His presence in my life and my ministry as the Teacher, the Director, the Instructor, and the Leader.

Thank you Lord for making me the lady evangelist with a unique anointing for teaching the prophetic-deliverance ministration with signs and wonders. I love you Lord, and I surrender my all to You. Amen!

This book is specially dedicated to the Caribbean, that the conviction of sin unto repentance will come upon the people of the West Indies. And that they will overcome religious spirits and surrender their all to the Lord Jesus Christ. Amen!

Contents

Foreword

Who is afraid to give the devil a show down? Jesus cast out devils as he healed the sick. Jesus also gave power and authority to his disciples to heal all manner of sicknesses and diseases and to also cast out devils. However, for many centuries, the Church seems to have departed from these unique aspects of ministry that engages the devil in spiritual warfare. Thank God for revelation. Our generation is here to recapture the Acts of the Apostles and put the devil where he belongs.

It is important for every one that claims allegiance to the Lordship of Jesus Christ to stand up to the task of knowing and understanding. Like a cankerworm, ignorance is a disease that eats up the sensitivity of the human body until destruction occurs. Not knowing can be as dangerous as fighting a cankerworm. The Church needs to get out of complacency to tackle the enemy in a war that will expose the tactics of deception.

In this book – *Receive and Maintain Your Deliverance on Legal Grounds*, Pauline has exposed the realms of captivity in which the enemy engages the people of God in all manner of warfare. She reveals the fact that the battle of life is not limited to just a little aspect of human endeavors, but in all realms, including the spiritual, physical, material, emotional and secular. Each chapter focuses on the type of captivity that humans face in a particular realm of the spirit and also provides the dozier for solution.

Indeed, this is a handbook for ministers and everyone who desires to understand reasons and importance of deliverance ministration. Every Christian deserves to know. The knowledge provided in this book will move the body of Christ into a new dimension of ministration with Biblical demonstrations as recorded in the New Testament; therefore I recommend it to all.

By: Greg Mauro
Vice President
Morris Cerullo World Evangelism

Poetic Expression

HE IS MY DELIVERER

The Lord is my deliverer
His delivering power is my freedom
Freedom from the chain that binds me
His delivering power is my liberty
Liberty from the chain of slavery
Indeed He is my deliverer

The Lord is my deliverer
His delivering power is my salvation
Salvation from transgression
His delivering power is my redemption
Redemption from iniquities
Indeed He is my deliverer

The Lord is my deliverer
His delivering power sets me free
And I am free from bondage
His delivering power breaks every yoke
And I am released from captivity
Indeed He is my deliverer

Dr. Pauline Walley, November, 1996

Introduction

W hen the Lord God created the heaven and earth, He enriched them with great wealth. Then He set up the Garden of Eden on earth. The Garden was an example of the wealth and prosperity that He intended mankind to inherit. Thus the Garden was blessed with rivers of living water in which there were fishes for food; animals and birds for meat; plants, herbs, vegetables and fruits for additional food; and silver, gold, onyx, and diamond for wealth. In addition to physical wealth, God also blessed mankind with His awesome presence, power, authority and dominion over the earth. He visited Adam and Eve in the Garden at certain hours of the day ("in the cool of the day"). However, the Lord God gave a command to mankind, not to touch a particular tree nor to eat from its fruit. He said, **"Of every tree of the Garden you may freely eat; but of the tree of the knowledge of good and evil you shall not eat, for in the day that you eat of it you shall surely die."** Mankind refused to obey this simple instruction. Instead of avoiding the tree and staying away from disobedience, mankind decided to go close and admire it. The closer he went, the more curious he became, and the more he was tempted to touch it.

One day, the deceiver noticed the interest that mankind had developed toward the tree of life. So he came closer and began to chat nicely with mankind. After a long chat, the deceiver succeeded in convincing mankind and lured him into disobedience. Hence the spirit of disobedience captured mankind, and he lost all the great wealth with which he was originally blessed by God to Satan the deceiver. Thus Satan stole away the power and authority that God had given to mankind, and replaced them with sin and death. He also stole the material wealth and made mankind poor. He stole the physical wealth and gave mankind sickness and weakness; **"For the thief cometh not but to steal, to kill, and to destroy...."**

After mankind's disobedience, a curse was placed upon him, and he lost the ability to subdue the earth. Hence, mankind was driven out of the Garden of Eden because of that one single sin of disobedience. This simply means that *only one sin is enough for one to go to hell.*

If just one error caused mankind to lose the presence of God, then everybody needs to know that a person does not need more than one sin to get into hell, just as one single passport or identity card is needed for an international traveler to enter into another nation. Similarly, just as man lost all his possessions when he was driven out of the Garden of Eden, so does a person lose his possessions whenever he is deported or repatriated out of a country. One loses everything that he ever acquired because of that action of deportation. Only restoration can get one back on track.

Not long after Adam and Eve had been driven out of the Garden, their son Cain also heeded the voice of Satan, despite previous warnings from God. He ignored the warning and went ahead to fulfill the desires of his heart. Although God gave him an opportunity to repent, he rejected it. Why—because he had inherited the sin of disobedience as well as the curse from his parents. The seed of this sort of inheritance can only be broken through deliverance ministration. Deliverance ministration is one of the major solutions that stubborn-hearted persons need to get rid of bad behavior.

Just as God's endowed authority was stolen from mankind when he was tempted in the Garden of Eden, so was it returned to humans when Jesus overcame the temptation in the wilderness when He was confronted by Satan after a 40-day fast, following His baptism by John the Baptist in the River Jordan. The authority for deliverance from Satan's captivity was finally released to mankind when the Lord Jesus was nailed upon the cross, and went down to the grave (through His burial) and rose up from death (by His resurrection). The purpose of the death and resurrection of Jesus Christ portrays the intention of what this book is about. Deliverance ministration is a curious issue that has attracted controversy from generation to generation since the days of Jesus Christ until the present age.

This book, *Receive and Maintain Your Deliverance on Legal Grounds* is not just another write-up, but the reality of my daily encounter with issues that attract a type of attention that should be described as *deliverance ministration.* It is a detailed compilation of my teachings and counseling on deliverance. Therefore it is meant to be complementary to my ministrations.

I have traveled around from one country to another, and my encounters in Europe, the Caribbean, Africa, Asia and America have revealed that all humans are vulnerable. Everyone is subject to demonic attack and demonic control, no matter who one is or where a person comes from or what one does. Satan the deceiver has managed to penetrate everywhere and is holding many in bondage and captivity. The solution to the various problems that people face all over the world is rooted in the Lord Jesus Christ. One of the major solutions that God has designed for us is *deliverance ministration.*

This book tackles some of the problems that need the application of deliverance ministration. My first book, ***The Authority of an Overcomer: You can have it...I have it*** and the second, ***Somebody Cares...Cares for you...Cares for me*** will give you basic understanding of some of the teachings on ***deliverance ministration***. The various instances cited are from real life encounters as shared by the persons involved. Some of the names have been changed for confidentiality, while others have been retained because the persons involved gave me their permission as their own personal contributions toward the advancement of the gospel of our Lord Jesus Christ.

This book will help you to understand deliverance and the reasons Christians must submit to deliverance ministration. It is divided into nine chapters. Each chapter will enlighten you on various types of captivity and bondages, and how to be set free from them. Each chapter opens with a poetic expression. The poems are meant to give the reader a prayer language that will help a person to renounce some of the things that have entangled one's life.

Chapter One opens with a general discussion on what people think about deliverance ministration, and why it is a controversial matter that attracts curiosity.

Chapter Two discusses the various reasons Christians must submit to deliverance ministration.

Chapter Three reveals how some biblical personalities lost their relationship with the Lord because of demonic contamination.

Chapter Four, Five, and Six reveal some of the things that contaminate our spiritual lives.

Chapter Seven shows us how to fight against the various issues that contaminate our Christian lives.

Chapters Eight and Nine also teach us how to manage broken hearts and hurts as well as how to retain the deliverance we need.

Poetic Expression One

THE THOUGHT OF DELIVERANCE

Why deliverance, why deliverance?
The thought bothers me
And I asked,
Have I not been saved?
Yes, saved but struggling with sin
Am I not devoted?
Yes, devoted but religiously traditional
Could the answer be deliverance?
Yes, deliverance is the answer.

The thought of deliverance
Overwhelms me
Is it a threat to my salvation?
Is it an answer to my problems?
Is it a strange phenomenon?
No, it is a reality.
Could it be the new dimension to prayer?
Yes, deliverance is the answer.

The thought of deliverance
Is a thought of prayer.
It is a thought of warfare,
Warring against the enemy.
It is the weapon of threat;
Threat to the kingdom of darkness
The thought of deliverance brings hope,
Hope to the frustrated.

Pauline Walley, November, 1996

Chapter One

THE CONTROVERSY:
Is Deliverance Ministration
A Myth Or A Reality?

W hen a portion of Scripture becomes controversial, what shall we do? The term *deliverance ministration* is comprised of two controversial words. Both Bible scholars and laymen are unclear as to what deliverance is all about. Some consider it a myth; some see it as a dramatic display of magical powers; some think it is a psychological trick on the mind. The controversy can also be observed even among those who declare acceptance of its reality. There is a lot of confusion because of the misrepresentation of what deliverance seeks to achieve. It has been hotly debated to the extent that even the House of Commons, the "reverend gentlemen" and the "theological scholars," have been given the assignment to research the furor.

This is not the first time a Biblical matter has tickled the mind of the House of Commons. The Methodist Church of the Wesleys was a departure from the Church of England because of the difficulty in accepting the word "salvation" and the phrase "Ye must be born again." Once again, the

Aristocrats and the scholars are at it, to agree and disagree with the term*deliverance*. Quite recently the House of Commons was debating the reality of healing miracles being carried out at the Morris Cerullo's annual crusades known as *Mission to London*. A group of disabled lots had called for the restraint of Morris Cerullo's ministration to those who desperately needed restoration. Unfortunately for the protestors, their demonstration rather attracted greater attendance, hope, and rising responses to the crusade. People travel from all over the world to participate and receive healing and miracles from *Mission to London.*

While the Mission to London's controversy is gradually being accepted as Biblically proven, the issue of deliverance has suddenly emerged. There is a great need to state the matter in a simplified manner, for a better understanding, and also to put the term *deliverance* where it belongs, or else it becomes a `dangling modifier' on the lips of users. Just as the Methodists are now cold toward the term *born again,* it may happen that the good impact of deliverance could be overlooked, and the matter sent into the doldrums.

However, the issue at hand is not based on the understanding of the actual meaning of deliverance ministration, but rather, how the term is being used, the scenario and the episode that some practitioners dramatize in modern times. Another fact is that the term is now being associated with some class of race and people from certain parts of the world. This sort of classification and sectionalism increases the controversial issues already at stake.

Interestingly, the ministry of the Lord Jesus Christ whom we seek to follow was also besieged with controversy. The Pharisees accused Him of casting out demons with the power of Beelzebub, which is the name of a principality of darkness. If the Messiah Himself faced such attacks, who can ward it off for praise?

Like the Pharisees, some brethren professing to be

Christ-like are desperately seeking defense for the office of the Messiah - the Christ, and in their "righteousness" may be seeking self-favor for popularity while in the process of putting their theology aright. If well examined, it will be discovered that the controversy is not actually based on the word *deliverance*, but on the methodology of ministration. It is the fact that the scene could be frightful and sometimes disturbing to onlookers. This book will endeavor to discuss some of the controversial issues that surround deliverance ministration. Here, we will look at the vivid meaning of the word *deliverance*, and how real it operates and is applicable to the issues to which it is being attached.

UNDERSTANDING DELIVERANCE MINISTRATION

The simple meaning of the word *deliverance* is "to set free." The spiritual application of freedom is "to cast out." The key word for deliverance is freedom. Other extensive descriptions of the word *deliverance* include: liberation, release, being loosed, redemption, and salvation.

Freedom in deliverance implies that a person who is constrained or limited by a situation has been granted emancipation. The restriction that demands freedom is known as bondage or captivity because it places a limitation on a person's ability to rise up and function either normally or effectively.

A person held in captivity may be restrained from moving around. Such a person may be bonded by fetters, shackles, and chains or by any kind of regulation. Just like a colt tied up to a tree is limited in its movement to the length of the chains, so is a person held in detention, imprisonment, or in any form of incarceration limited to the confinement of the prison walls which is a type of bondage, and would usually want to be set free.

There are various forms of captivity that need different forms of deliverance, such as spiritual captivity, physical captivity, material captivity, financial captivity, emotional captivity, and secular captivity. One form of captivity may lead to another. Captivities are usually connected. A person held in spiritual captivity may be vulnerable to all other forms of captivities.

<u>Liberation</u> in deliverance has to do with being released from rules, regulations, restrictions or doctrines that oppress or suppress by hindering people from thinking beyond a belief system. Sometimes people belong to organizations or associations whose doctrines hinder or limit the individuals from functioning as normal human beings. Some laws imposed by such organizations create segregation and sectionalism.

For instance, there are men whose opinion about women is impassionate. In view of that, they formulate doctrines that restrict the ability of women, whereby women are limited in their ability to perform important roles that fulfill their destiny, despite the fact that they are created to be help-mates and not slaves nor second-class citizens.

Also, there are certain organizations that uphold rules and regulations that create sectionalism and racism or a type of class strata that oppress or suppress the minority. Some of these human violations may be caused by some spiritual entities. Therefore, deliverance is eminent.

<u>Release</u> in deliverance means to disentangle a person from an oath or a promise that has a spiritual implication or some form of repercussion. Such oaths and promises include covenant, vows and pledges. The implication or repercussion involved could be deadly or may lead to involuntary transference of evil spirits or inheritance of curses.

Out of desperation and ignorance, many people have taken oaths or made promises that have tied them up to relationships that are no longer fruitful or profitable. It also means that a person is in a type of relationship that is binding. Sometimes people are involved in societies or associations that require secret initiation, whereby oaths are sworn and covenants or vows are enacted.

There are cases where pronouncements and declarations made by people in authority can affect innocent individuals because they may constitute a curse if it has legal grounds. Such pronouncements and declarations need to be broken or reversed in order for victims to be released.

Loose in deliverance implies that a person tied up or bound up with physical or spiritual rope needs to be set free. It could also mean that a person is held captive in a cage like a bird and the cage is locked up with a physical or spiritual padlock.

In some traditions, people are tied down with rope to a monument or a tree as a form of punishment, while in certain traditions, the dead is bound up in white raiment before burial just as indicated in the case of Lazarus. Binding is also an occultic practice whereby an image or a photograph or an effigy made to represent an individual is bound up in the spiritual realm so that physically that individual will not be able to make progress in life. Victims held by situations related to these categories need to be loosed.

Salvation in deliverance is the act of being salvaged from satanic invasion and demonic interference. Through warfare individuals facing danger or satanic terrorism can be saved or delivered from satanic atrocities.

Redemption in deliverance is to recover from a generational curse. It means to risk one's life to rescue another life from perishing.

Deliverance is a descriptive word for the act of casting out devils, setting the captive free, setting loose from bondage as indicated in

Luke 4:18-19,

The Spirit of the Lord is upon Me, Because He has anointed Me to preach the gospel to the poor; He has sent Me to heal the broken-hearted. To proclaim liberty [deliverance] to the captives And recovery of sight to the blind, To set at liberty those who are oppressed, To proclaim the acceptable year of the Lord. (*Words in brackets by author.*)

Based on the various meanings given, it is adequate to state that deliverance ministration is intended to get rid of demonic character, behavior and attitude that depict the nature of man, and cause him to lead an unworthy lifestyle. Deliverance ministration is intended to shake off the shackles of burdens that demoralize a person from progressing. It is a means of breaking loose from the influence of occultic practices. It is meant to tear asunder the bonds of illegal or demonic covenant with persons or agents of the enemy.

In essence, deliverance is total salvation from sin and corruption from satanic ideas, demonic concept, demonic behavior and demonic standards. It is a means of cleansing oneself from pollution and corruption of the body, soul, spirit and mind.

Deliverance is to set free a person held in spiritual bondage or captivity through supernatural means, especially by the power in the name of Jesus Christ the Redeemer. Deliverance ministration requires a supernatural endowment (anointing) and the intervention of the presence of the Holy Spirit. It also requires the consent or permission of the Almighty God because it is a spiritual warfare.

In the Old Testament days, deliverance was administered through the process of purification and sanctification carried out by the High Priests and members of the Levites. Details of these are discussed in the subsequent chapters.

WHAT IS THE DIFFERENCE BETWEEN DELIVERANCE AND SALVATION?

One of the questions that has been the cause of controversy is the difficulty of differentiating between deliverance ministration and declaration of accepting Jesus as Lord and Savior of one's life. After all, deliverance also means to save—salvation from sin. The purpose of confessing Jesus as Lord and Savior is for one to be set free from the act of disobedience and sin.

The term, "born-again" is the act of making a declaration to surrender one's life to Jesus, and to accept the Lordship of Jesus Christ over one's life. It is a new birth into the realm of the Holy Spirit, for the purpose of a Spirit-controlled life to replace the birth of the flesh, which is easily controlled by the prince of this world—Satan. This declaration is the initial decision that leads one into a new realm of life in Christendom. Having entered the realm, there are other steps that one has to take that will ascertain the initial decision.

One of the major steps is for one to study the rules and regulations of the Kingdom of God. Ignorance of these facts will nullify the initial decision, because without a deep knowledge of Jesus Christ, it will be difficult for one to accept His Lordship in reality. It will also be difficult for one to walk in obedience to His word.

Accepting His Lordship means to seek and to accept His control, direction and leadership. The rules and regulations to be studied constitute the complete Word of God, the Holy Scriptures in the Holy Bible. The Old Testament should not be ignored, for without it, the Word of God would be incomplete. One cannot understand the end, if one does not know what the foundation or beginning is. The beginning must come for there to be an end.

More so, the details of deliverance are well spelled out in the Old Testament. The problem that many people have with "truth" is that, they never take time to study the whole truth. They are only interested in the portions of Scripture that suit them. Along the line of study, biblical rules and regulations are expected to be made applicable to one's life. Without the application, the initial confession will be vague. The essence of the Word of God is to prune, correct, instruct and direct as indicated in

2 Timothy 3:16-17,

All Scripture is given by inspiration of God, and is profitable for doctrine, for reproof, for correction, for instruction in righteousness, that the man of God may be complete, thoroughly equipped for every good work.

During the process of studying, one must endeavor to accept corrections accordingly. The Scripture is the Word of God unto us. Each time we set out to read or study, the Lord is called upon to speak to us through His Word. Studying the Scriptures diligently is like standing in the presence of God to receive instruction. Therefore we should not despise any portion of the Scripture, thinking that it refers to another. God deserves all the respect, and so we need to relax our heart and mind and accept the truth that the Scripture points to in our lives, and make instant adjustment.

Philippians 2:12-13 admonishes us,

**...Work out your own salvation with fear
and trembling; for it is God who works in
you both to will and to do for His good
pleasure.**

It is during the process of studying that one will notice
some characteristics that seem too difficult to do away
with. Such could include anger, deception, lies, lust,
fornication, adultery, drunkenness, dissensions and
contentions. Some of these characteristics could be prevalent in a family (hereditary sin). Usually, when a characteristic is a common trait in a family, then one could be
dealing with demonic oppression and principalities of
darkness. In such a case where a characteristic persists in
one's life, despite all efforts made to renounce it, then
there will be a need for the assistance of *"a man of God"*
to intercede for one.

Cleansing and Washing

When such a case arises in a person's life, after declaration of having been born again, then there is need for the
domineering spirit in charge of that devilish character to be
cast out. The act of casting out devils from a person's life
can be referred to as deliverance ministration.

In some other cases, there are people who suffer from all
sorts of demonic oppressions that do not necessarily affect
their character, but have to do with infirmities or mysterious
attacks caused by the agents of Satan and some forces of
darkness. The act of commanding the oppressing forces to
cease operation in such people's lives is referred to as deliverance ministration. (Details of this will be found in the
subsequent chapters.)

It is pertinent to state that the act of confessing and accepting Jesus Christ as Lord and Savior is not a guarantee for achieving total "salvation" instantly. It is a process of ushering one's life into seeking the salvation of one's soul, which is done on a daily basis, as one grows and matures in the things of God; backed by a strong foundation on the Holy Scriptures.

Please note that dipping a dirty cloth inside a bucket of water, does not guarantee a clean wash, unless detergent is added and washing is made with the hands to ensure that all stains are removed. For a good look, some clothes will need ironing else, one will appear rough and unpresentable.

> **Ephesians 5:25-27 states, Christ also loved the church and gave Himself for it, that He might sanctify and cleanse it with the washing of water by the word, that He might present it to Himself a glorious church, not having spot or wrinkle or any such thing, but that it should be holy and without blemish.**

There is therefore a crucial need for persons who surrender their lives to Christ to be encouraged to work out their salvation with the effort of studying the Holy Scriptures.

Colossians 3:16-17 states,

> **Let the word of Christ dwell in you richly in all wisdom, teaching and admonishing one another... And whatever you do in word, or deed, do all in the name of the Lord Jesus, giving thanks to God the Father through Him.**

Obviously, we need to sort ourselves out of the issues of life that entangle us in sin. We need deliverance from the things that cause the soiling of our robes with blemishes and also attract our past vomit. However, we must note that deliverance is not limited to casting out devils; sometimes counseling could bring healing and deliverance to our souls.

Studying the Word of God has a greater impact in the deliverance of the soul, rather than shouting or screaming prayer. This is why some people struggle with sleep each time they make attempts to read the Holy Bible. Some can hardly read the Scriptures for a period of ten minutes, before a heavy sleep will fall upon them; or they will be distracted by issues that are not particularly necessary at the moment. Unless the controlling force is rebuked, such a one may never hear or understand the Scriptures. The inability to read and understand the Scriptures can hinder one's relationship with the Lord Jesus Christ. The more you study the Scriptures, the better you discover who He is, and the stronger your faith and foundation in the Lord becomes. Salvation and deliverance are siblings; they operate together in one accord.

THE MINISTRY OF JESUS AND DELIVERANCE MINISTRATION

The Lord Jesus Christ was quite aware of the need for deliverance. Deliverance ministration was very much pronounced in the ministry of Jesus Christ. In the four gospels of the New Testament, it was recorded that Jesus healed the sick of all manner of disease, cleansed the lepers, cast out devils and worked innumerable miracles; most of which were not recorded.

Matthews 8:16-17 states,

When evening had come, they brought to Him many who were demon-possessed. And He cast out the spirits with a word, and healed all who were sick, that it might be fulfilled which was spoken by Isaiah the prophet, saying: "He Himself took our infirmities and bore our sicknesses."

This account reveals that the issue of demonic oppression, suppression, and possession is not a myth, but a reality. Whatever Jesus did was done because we need not be ignorant of the truth of the things in this life. The outstanding truth about the ministry of Jesus, which the controversies have failed to address, is: Why should we neglect the poor and the needy? Of what benefit will it have been if the demon-possessed are left to roam the streets without care and cure? Who is that parent who takes delight in watching his or her child go crazy and will deny such a one the necessary attention? It is obviously a great joy to everyone who might have witnessed the deliverance of the mad man of Gergesenes recorded in

Matthew 8:28-34,

When He had come to the other side, to the country of the Gergesenes, there met Him two demon-possessed men, coming out of the tombs, exceedingly fierce, so that no one could pass that way. And suddenly they cried out, saying, "What have we to do with You, Jesus, You Son of God? Have You come here to torment us before the time?" Now a good way off

from them there was a herd of many swine feeding. So the demons begged Him, saying, "If You cast us out, permit us to go away into the herd of swine." And He said to them, "Go." So when they had come out, they went into the herd of swine, ran violently down the steep place into the sea, and perished in the water. Then those who kept them fled; and they went away into the city and told everything, including what had happened to the demon-possessed men. And behold, the whole city came out to meet Jesus. And when they saw Him, they begged Him to depart from their region."

Imagine the violent attitude of the two men whose lives were, at that time, a great loss to their families. The situation of a madman can sometimes be compared to that of a "dead body;" that was why they retired to the graveyard, in anticipation of death. Another issue is that the human body is not meant to be a habitation of demons and other satanic agents. The body is meant to be the temple of the living God. So the possession of demons is illegal trespassing; they must be ejected immediately. The demons were quite aware of this fact; that was why they begged Jesus not to destroy them before their time. In fact they (the demons) asked for permission to abide in the swine.

Please note that demons have various ranks and areas of operations. All demons are not violent, and all are not related to madness. Therefore one cannot attribute every demonic case to action noted in people. For instance, in another incident involving demonic operation, it was noted that there was no violence involved...

Matthew 9:32-34,

As they went out, behold, they brought to Him a man, mute and demon-possessed. And when the demon was cast out, the mute spoke. And the multitudes marveled, saying, "It was never seen like this in Israel!" But the Pharisees said, "He casts out demons by the ruler of the demons."

Also, in **Matthew 12:22-24 it says,**

Then one man was brought to Him who was demon-possessed, blind and mute; and He healed him so that the blind and mute man both saw and spoke. And all the multitudes were amazed and said, "Could this be the Son of David?" But when the Pharisees heard it they said, "This fellow does not cast out demons except by Beelzebub, the ruler of the demons."

It is pertinent to note that there is always a controversy whenever Jesus cast out devils. After the two madmen had been set free, the people living in the region did not want Jesus to continue such type of ministration. It was strange to them. Instead of appreciation, they became bitter. They were more interested in keeping their herds of swine, rather than having the men delivered.

In the case of the mute child, people were ready to sympathize with the parents, rather than rejoice over his deliverance. In view of that, words of discouragement were uttered to hurt Jesus. More than the accusation is the fact that people attach the results of great works of mystery to Satan the deceiver, instead of giving the acknowledgment to

God the Creator of heaven and earth. What power has the devil and his agents that were not given to them? God is able to give and redeem whatever power the enemy possesses to oppress. Having come as an example, Jesus did not only demonstrate the methodology through which salvation could be attained by all men, but also taught the disciples to carry out the same.

Matthew 10:1 says,

And when He had called His twelve disciples to Him, He gave them power over unclean spirits, to cast them out, and to heal all kinds of sickness and all kinds of disease.

When He later sent them out to practice what they had been taught, Jesus stressed the need to demonstrate the authority given to them.

Matthew 10:5-8 says,

These twelve Jesus sent out and commanded them, saying; "...Heal the sick, cleanse the lepers, raise the dead, cast out demons. Freely you have received, freely give." Casting out devils is part of the 'Great Commission' that Jesus gave to His disciples.

It is a command to be carried out, and must not be neglected. Demonic attack is a strategy that the enemy uses to gain followers. Satan attacks the mind, the intellect, the heart, the soul, the spirit and any other part of the human body through which he can gain legal operation.

The Controversy in the World of Deliverance
(An excerpt from *Foursquare Mirror* by Pauline Walley)

On several occasions, before the resumption of a deliverance service at a certain Foursquare Gospel Church, in an attempt to usher in people waiting around the premises, I often asked, "Please, are you here for deliverance service?" Many of these people have reacted sharply as if the question was offensive. "I'm not for deliverance, oh, I'm for healing." Sometimes, the manner in which the reply was presented prompted me to ask the second question, "*What is the difference between deliverance and healing?*" Of course, my inquiry never got any further response...

The most pathetic aspect of the controversy hinges on the fact that some brethren believe in what the devil can do, more than in what the power of God can do. Just like the Pharisees accused Jesus of casting out the devil of dumbness with the power of Beelzebub (the chief of the devils, **Luke 11:14-15**), so do many brethren make accusation today.

Deliverance is total salvation. It is one of the signs of wonders that follow immediately upon one deciding to accept Jesus Christ as Lord and Savior. It is supposed to be done instantly because the Holy Spirit, who takes over when a person confesses Christ, cannot dwell in the heart where there is an unclean spirit.

Salvation means being taken out of a sinful world. That was why Jesus told Nicodemus in **John 3:1-16** that except a man be born of water and the Spirit, he cannot enter into the kingdom of God. Jesus took the pains to explain the meaning of, and reasons for, being born again in this passage. The passage implies that a man needs to be brought out completely from the former state in which he lived.

Therefore, to step out from the sinful nature which is polluted and filthy, a dwelling place for the devil's agents—such as spirits of lying, gossip, murder, envy, strife, self-centeredness, self-righteousness, religious spirits, etc, one has to be ministered to. The ministration can be done successfully if the intending convert confesses his involvement in the world.

The act of deliverance ministration is like a sick man who consults a medical doctor for treatment. During the consultation the sick man opens up and tells the physician all that is wrong with him so that the sickness can be diagnosed adequately. The medical doctor sometimes digs into the medical history of the patient, to enable him to determine the appropriate solution to the ailment. If the medical doctor proves inefficient in the initial approach to the patient's treatment, the sickness is bound to reoccur and sometimes much more seriously. In some cases, the patient may then be referred to a specialist. Sometimes the patient on his own may change doctors, and the patient may deteriorate due to the inefficiency of the first physician who treated him.

Similarly, the work of salvation is just like that of the physician. Christians need deliverance because many did not surrender their spiritual soul-tie and covenant to Jesus when they first met Him. Since the minister involved in a particular case was probably not equipped for deliverance ministration, or ignorant of the signs and wonders that are needed to take place immediately after confession of sin was made, that convert now has to seek spiritual medication, which is deliverance.

The Bible reveals that Jesus ministered full salvation unto men, unlike the "half-baked" sermons preached in many pulpits by some people today. During ministrations, Jesus ensured that the individuals involved were set free from all evil powers surrounding their lives; including sickness, deformation, insanity, blindness, deafness, dumbness, poverty, etc., which are all linked to and are signs of demonic possession. Jesus' ministration was a combination of purifi-

35

cation and sanctification which ensured total salvation. A newborn baby is really new in the hands of Jesus. That was why he said to Nicodemus, "Ye must be born again." It is part of the reason Jesus gave power to the disciples when He sent them out on assignment as part of their training:

The Bible says in Luke 9:1-9,

Then He called his twelve disciples together, and gave them power and authority over all devils, and to cure diseases. And He sent them to preach the kingdom of God, and heal the sick.

During the second errand recorded in **Luke 10**, the disciples returned with the report that "Even the devils are subject unto us through thy name [the name of Jesus]." In **Acts 1**, Jesus enjoined the disciples to wait for the promise of the Father so that they could bear witness of Him. It was also discovered that some time after delivering people from whatever problems they suffered, Jesus did make utterances like "Go and sin no more," "Your sins are forgiven". An instance is recorded in **Luke 5:17-26**, when Jesus healed a man with paralysis.

Some of these passages reveal that the causes of infirmities are largely attributed to sins committed consciously or unconsciously. Some sicknesses are recurrent, while some demons involved could only be provoked to manifestation at maturity or specific times and seasons.

As soon as a man decides to surrender his life to Jesus, having said the sinner's prayer, his past life must be buried with a total confession of his involvement in the world; especially where there have been cases of occultism. The confession will enable him to be delivered totally from all powers of the devil in his life. Then such a person can boldly step into the kingdom of God as a truly saved sinner. Ministering repentance to people without the signs of being delivered from spiritual problems instantly has brought about the need for a different approach to deliverance ministrations. In order to make people feel free to complete the process of salvation, various names are given to ministration centers, such as: **Faith Clinic, Power House, Miracle Service, Power Line, Spiritual Clinic,** etc. This leads one to ask the question, *"Who needs deliverance?"*

WHO NEEDS DELIVERANCE MINISTRATION?

As said earlier, many people make confessions and repentance with their lips, while the heart is heavy with sin. Many such persons live in the church and act as agents of the devil, because their salvation was not completed at the initial stage. The religious spirit takes them over and gives them the endurance of living under the rules of **dos** and **don'ts**. They live by good works in the church by the aid of the religious demons. That is why you discover that dynamic workers like Ushers, Choristers, Sunday School Workers, Church Drivers and Altar Workers and some ministers are forced to go for deliverance under the pretext of minor body ailment. Most of them go for their ministration *"nicodemously."*

Deliverance ministration is meant for anyone who professes Jesus Christ as Lord and Savior for the completion of the work of salvation. That is why **Philippians 2:12-13** encourages us to **"Work out your own salvation with fear and trembling."** Without deliverance, a supposed believer lives in turbulent waters, jumping from one problem into the other. They are fond of making complaints always, submitting prayer requests, and lack the joy and peace of the Lord in their lives.

Deliverance is the cleansing that a Christian needs to ensure that his life is sanctified, purified and habitable for the Holy Spirit. As much as the Bible is for the born-again believers, so is deliverance for believers, because deliverance is cleansing of the soul and spirit from contrary spirits.

If Christians are free to claim the promise of God, then they must be ready to accept whatever He says in totality. On no grounds does the Word of God belong to unbelievers. A non-Christian certainly has no inheritance in God. He is a potential Christian, but until he declares for Christ and goes through total salvation, his life is on the line, and he has the devil as his father. The same goes for a supposed believer who knows that his spiritual life is not purified. Even sincerely born-again Christians often need cleansing, which is deliverance. This is because Christians do get contaminated and if deliverance is not sought, it can lead to spiritual coldness and backsliding. Once saved is not forever saved.

TRUTH IS BITTER, BUT IT'S JUST THE TRUTH,
AND GOD IS TRUTH.

Poetic Expression Two

WAR AGAINST IGNORANCE

War against ignorance
Yes, I have heard
That ignorance is not just a word
But a disease, a cankerworm
It could destroy the soul
It could kill
Nay, I shall no longer tolerate it
I shall no longer abide with it
I shall arise
And I shall war against ignorance

War against ignorance
Nay, I shall no longer admit you
Neither shall I walk with you
You are not my friend
Neither are you my neighbor
Get thee behind me
You intend to destroy my life
But today, you have been exposed
Yes, I shall war against ignorance

War against ignorance
Get thee out of my soul
Get thee out of my spirit and flesh
Get thee out of my thought
I shall no longer keep thy companion
I break every covenant I have with thee
Disappear from my presence
Leave me alone

I have conquered you
Yes, I have overcome ignorance.

Pauline Walley, November 1996.

Chapter Two

DO CHRISTIANS NEED DELIVERANCE?

The controversy surrounding deliverance may never get exhausted until Jesus returns. Despite the discussions so far from the previous chapter, one may still need an in-depth explanation on the issue of deliverance ministration. This chapter and the subsequent ones will endeavor to cite real life circumstances involving some persons who are devoted to the things of God in the House of God, and yet had to seek deliverance before they could achieve their breakthrough. Testimonies of persons who have experienced deliverance after salvation will be cited to help others to understand the issue being discussed.

As mentioned earlier on, deliverance ministration is actually meant for Christians—such persons who have renounced the control of Satan and the cares of this world for fellowship with Jesus Christ our Lord and Savior. Having made a confession to accept Jesus Christ as one's Lord, the next step to be taken is to repossess one's life from satanic control, through the act of deliverance. At this point, the chains of captivity have to be broken to set the person free. If there be any property of Satan deposited in the person's life, especially persons once involved in occultism of some sort, such properties have to be sent out by the blood of Jesus and the physical properties be destroyed.

INHERITANCE

There are various things that we inherit from members of our families and relatives that could entangle our lives. These include material/financial wealth, spiritual wealth, and behavioral attitude. As much as some of these inheritances are great and good, some are also demonic and destructive. This discussion will focus on the inheritances that entangle and destroy people's virtues, the details of which will be found in subsequent chapters—Spiritual, Physical and Material captivities, respectively.

THE HUMAN CHARACTER AND BEHAVIORIAL ATTITUDE

Childhood Traits

It is often a great joy to describe a child as a replica of the parents in terms of physical appearance. However, it is a problem to attribute the bad behavior of a child to the parents as no one takes delight in being referred to as "badly behaved."

Most often children turn to behave the same way they see their parents perform. They learn from watching, and it is their pleasure to copy and practice what they see and live with every day. Therefore, the quarrels that go on between parents, the outburst of wrath from angered parents, the corrupt conversation, the intolerance and unaccommodating attitude, the unhealthy environment under which children are brought up do affect their future. Thus, these behaviors are often copied and carried over from generation to generation.

In view of this, some common traits are peculiar with some family lineage. These common traits could be peculiar, yet they may be bad ones. For instance, in a family where outbursts of wrath exist, the majority of the people in that family are hot-tempered, easily infuriated over petty issues, lack understanding, lack communication flow; all the manifestations attached to outbursts of wrath are distributed among members of the family.

Every child born to such a family would be controlled by this peculiar inheritance in character. Since an outburst of wrath is demonic, being a work of the flesh **(Galatians 5:20)**, if the family concerned does not seek deliverance against it, but accommodates it as being a family trait or family characteristic, then the principalities of darkness will ask a special demon to control that family, and influence them to demonstrate this character from generation to generation. Therefore, no one talks about it and everyone will be content with it.

Divorce and Separation

Similarly, in a family where divorce has once been sanctioned, the spirit that controls marriage disunity and breakdown will begin to seek avenues to control such. This is why it is easy to find a woman with four to six children who belong to different fathers. In the same family, all the children may be suffering family breakdown such as separation from spouse (husband or wife), incessant quarrels and fighting, remarriages and sometimes sexual assault.

This is because divorce is influenced by a demonic spirit that causes sexual sins—adultery, fornication, uncleanness, licentiousness, incest, homosexuality, lesbianism, and such **(Galatians 5:19)**. One spirit attracts the other. Demons move in rank and file. They attack gradually through various means until they have gained full entrance and control over the life of an individual or group of persons.

For instance, people who come to me for counseling and deliverance ministration are given a form to complete. The form enables me to deal with the root of the problem that the individual is encountering. Sometimes, while going through the details of the history of a person's family, I realize that the problem is a family trait, being common in that person's family, and that has been passed on from generation to generation. Sometimes it is scattered, not quite regular, but does spring up once in a while. Some of such traits are associated with marriage, sickness/diseases, financial lack (poverty), struggling life/suffering, failure, disappointments, sorrow/pain, early deaths, blindness and many more.

A woman once told me that she would be better off if she lived apart from her husband. Then I asked, "Why do you think so, will your parents support this kind of idea?" She said, "No one in my family ever settled down in their marriage. My grandmother's mother had four children by four men. Only one of them got married, but later divorced. My grandmother had six children by four men. None of them actually settled down, although they had good proposals from wealthy men. My own mother also had five children by five men so each of us has a different father. In fact, I am the only one who has stayed with my marriage till this date. However, I find it hard to tolerate my husband."

According to her, she cannot tolerate the control of a man. She is a perfectionist, and wants everything around her to be exactly as she wants it to be. And her three daughters are already following her footsteps; the children do not want to be instructed by their father. They want to be left alone to do what pleases them.

After the interview, I pointed out to her that although she claims to be a Christian, and a leader in her church, who participates in major programs, she is still being controlled by the powers of darkness that control marriage. She has inherited a common trait in her family. Unconsciously, she has been yielding to the control of the demons in charge of divorce. Twice, she has had periods of separation, and twice her pastor has reunited her with her husband. The problems have always been considered as trivial and unnecessary. Yet this woman held strongly to her weakness.

I also made her realize that unless she submits herself to deliverance, and observes the portion of Scripture that encourages wives to submit to their husbands, her children will inherit the same spirit and weaknesses. Yet they will be claiming to have the Lordship of Jesus Christ. This is not normal and has to be checked. Jesus Christ is tolerant of us because of His love for all, but *His Lordship has no room for divorce, separation or broken homes.* These are attacks of Satan against the institution of marriage. God blessed the man and the woman, and said the two shall be one flesh. Therefore, no one should encourage marital breakdown or separation. Amen.

One of the major characters that affect broken homes is intolerance. The spirit of intolerance moves with impatience and inability to endure. Whenever spouses fail to work on their individual characters, but seek to blame one another for anything that happens in the home, the enemy will encourage breakdown in communication.

Romans 5:3-5 says,

...we glory in tribulations, knowing that tribulation produces perseverance; and perseverance, character; and character, hope. Now hope does not disappoint,

because the love of God has been poured out in our hearts by the Holy Spirit who was given to us.

Recently, I came across a man whose marriage is being influenced by his own mother. This man allows his mother to control his marriage negatively. Every now and then the mother will find out what has gone wrong between the two spouses and will encourage her son to punish the woman by returning home to her mother. At least, within a space of three months, the husband who is a Sunday School teacher, packed in and out of his marital home over petty misunderstandings that could be tackled quietly.

Although this man is a leader in his church where altar calls are made consistently to win souls for the Lord, yet he is not purged and refined. His character is far from being that of a responsible teacher whose life should be an example to the students he teaches. He cannot tolerate "the bone of his bone" and "the flesh of his flesh." He cannot endure the pain of the life in which he seeks to be one and united. How then can he lead others? How sincere is his Christianity? Does he actually submit to the Lordship of Jesus Christ or he is still bound by satanic control?

Therefore, as Christians we should examine our personal character and the common traits in our families and relations. Let us endeavor to get rid of them through deliverance ministration; otherwise we shall be making mockery of the Word of God.

For instance, my mother used to be very strict and militant in character. She demanded abrupt response to instructions. This was very taxing for me, and I almost hated her for it. During one of the times that I was interceding for her to change along with her new life in Jesus, the Lord pointed it out to me that I had begun to act and behave like my mother. He made me realize that if I did not purge my character, it would affect my ministry and Christian virtue. I sought deliverance ministration over all the character and behavioral attitudes that I had ever displayed in my life. I turned to the Scriptures and renounced all the works of the flesh known and unknown to me. This brought a tremendous change to my life. Once again I was revived, and the Lord blessed me.

When I took the initial step to seek deliverance, people thought I didn't mean it because I had been involved in deliverance ministration. But I insisted and told the minister that I wanted to get it right with God. And that I would not allow shame and disgrace to rob me of my blessings. *It took humility for me to overcome pride, which was one of the major characteristics that I needed to let go* in order for me to receive the fullness of His presence. (See details on characters under *Physical Captivity.*)

Material and Financial Wealth

Sometimes there is need for us to find out the source of the material wealth that we inherit. This is very necessary if such an inheritance has passed through more than one generation. If it is a direct inheritance from one's immediate parents, it is still necessary to find out some vital information regarding the foundation of such properties.

No matter how close you are to your parents, or how much you love the owner of the original properties, your love and closeness will not change the situation surrounding the property you have inherited until you have put your Christianity right. People are fond of dedicating their wealth, property, business, investments to something, somebody, or to gods, or to the Almighty God. Sometimes, the initial owner might have made covenants with some deities (demons/gods) or to the Almighty God, which need to be fulfilled.

There are cases where people celebrate some unusual occasions and make sacrifices to promote their wealth. Bearing all such happenings in mind, it is necessary to find out the source, investigate quietly, and renounce any association that will contaminate you. If you ignore the references and carry on, you will later face an encounter which you will not be able to bear. When the times become rough and tough, then you will remember that you have not formally claimed your authority over the spiritual environment, neither have you committed and dedicated the business to the Almighty God, and consecrated it with the blood of Jesus Christ. The material and financial wealth inherited must all be dedicated afresh, sometimes with prayer and fasting. Otherwise, some of these inheritances could affect one's relationship with God. It could cause one to backslide. It could be destructive. It could attract problems, family disunity, legal action, frustration and depression and such.

A man passed on his wealth and business organization to his children, and also to an occult society that he belonged to. He then told his children not to tamper with a standing contribution he makes to the occult. When one of his children who was a Christian objected, he threatened to bequeath half of his property to the occult to serve the same purpose. Then he stated that he was quite aware that the children might not be interested in participating in that society after his death; that was why he authorized the "standing order" through the bank, so that the business would not collapse.

This is a clear-cut example of demonic dedication at the source of the man's wealth. The foundation of the business was laid on occult covenant, and so the sacrifices must be made. Such a case needs divine intervention. If you are a Christian facing a similar problem with your inheritance, you need to summon the attention of deliverance ministers, to break the covenant and pull down the strongholds of the enemy around that property. Otherwise, you will be attacked, and the situation could be terrible. For we fight not against flesh and blood but against powers and principalities of darkness in high places.

IF THE PROPERTY YOU OCCUPY IS GHOST-HAUNTED, WHAT WILL YOU DO?

Barry Rattray *(Outlook Sunday Magazine*, Dec 24, 1995*)* reports that one of the great "dream" houses in Jamaica, in the Caribbean is ghost haunted. **The Norbrook Great House in Upper St. Andrew** was built by the Henderson family in the early 1940's. The formidable looking structure of 20,000 square feet of living space, now sits on four acres of manicured gardens, including a profusion of flowerbeds. It comprises seven separate large self-contained apartments, a cottage, and guard and maintenance accommodations.

High ceilings complement mahogany floors and paneled walls. Large concrete pillars stand tall, while huge windows stare at you. Solid walls over 12 inches thick attest to the might and strength of the castle and cellars mystify outsiders. The swimming pool cools the atmosphere.

Two "spirits" of vital importance to the castle live here with complete respect for each other. The one who is of the present is an international creative guru. The other "spirit" from the past (the haunting ghost), said to coexist here, is the infamous villainess Annie Palmer, who is credited with murdering her three husbands and a legacy of other atrocities...

But why is the white witch of Rose Hall so connected to this house? Why is it some visitors in absolute fear refuse to stay overnight here? Why? The fact is: This castle, basking in history and frightening legend, has Annie Palmer (claimed by many), appearing on her staircase every night protecting part of her possessions.

Many mansions are currently left unoccupied in various parts of the world because of this same reason of mystic presence—fright, fear and strange voices which are all demonic activities. If you were given this property for an inheritance, what would you do as a Christian? Would you dismiss the other person's experience as baseless and unfounded, or would you attack the situation? (See *Material Captivity* for details.)

SPIRITUAL AND RELIGIOUS WEALTH

One popular wealth that is commonly inherited all around the world is religion. Christianity and religion are inherited from birth. Where children are brought up with the beliefs of their parents, they are also trained to follow and worship according to the beliefs that the parents hold on to.

This system has increased the religious beliefs and traditional way of worship that exist in the denominational churches all over the world. In that, people do not strive to make efforts to seek the desire of the Almighty God in their worship system. They simply maintain to traditions that keep the Holy Spirit out of worship. And so as time goes on, the services become stereotyped and predictable, fixed and rigid. The children born into the system inherit the same and hold on to it as the religion of "our forefathers;" changing it would mean disobedience to authority, or heresy.

The Holy Spirit moves in diverse manners. He is unpredictable, and does things in His own way. Mankind cannot control or bottle Him; otherwise, His presence would be missing wherever He is not allowed to function.

Today, there are so many people bound up by religion. Such people are active and responsible in the denominational assemblies, especially in the old traditional churches. The religious people are used to the same old systems. They do not compromise with changes. The youth are not allowed to express their views. Rules and regulations are stringent. Doctrinal beliefs are strictly observed rather than the Holy Scriptures.

The religious spirit is demonic and destructive. It has kept most churches cold or lukewarm. It is a controlling spirit that entertains sin and works of the flesh. In a denomination where it exists, some members are involved in secret societies such as the Lodge, Rosicrucian, Witchcraft and Sorcery, Astrology, Crystal, Palm reading, New Age Spiritualism, Medium, Freemason and other cults around the world.

The religious spiritist preaches false holiness and emphasizes goodness to all creatures, including insects and animals. They suppress worship services and cause the members to feel depressed and frustrated. Some strict religious people transfer the wealth of their beliefs to their children in the form of inheritance. Some could disown members of the family who refuse to follow their personal beliefs.

There are Christians who do not believe that other denominational assemblies are of God, except the ones that they belong to. Such Christians do hold on to beliefs pertaining to physical appearance, rather than that which is spiritual. They hold on to doctrinal laws of "do's" and "don'ts," which people are afraid to break. These types of emphases are dangerous to the Christian faith, and do attract religious spirits.

A religious spirit is an oppressive demon that suppresses the joy of salvation. It holds its victims in bondage with rules and regulations that causes the fear of man rather than the fear of God. Any one person or organization operating under the influence of a religious spirit needs to seek liberation through deliverance ministration. Otherwise, one will be living in the shadows of Christianity, observing the laws of men rather than purifying the spirit against the works of the flesh. (See *Spiritual Captivity* for details.)

People involved in a secret society also transfer their occultic beliefs to their children. Before they die, sometimes they pass on their demonic powers through ornaments and jewels - rings, amulets, or keys (gold/silver). Demonic wealth is also transferred through meals and money – usually coins. Examine your inheritance, and be sincere about it. Don't think you are all right with it because it comes from a reputable person whom you hold in high esteem. You will surely be entangled by that precious gift before long. "Had I known" always comes at last, when it is too late for restoration. A word is sufficient to the wise.

ANCESTRAL WORSHIP AND HEROIC HONOR

One of the major battles that we frequently encounter in deliverance ministration is ancestral transference and inheritance that involves ancestral control and protection. Many individuals, both Christians and non-Christians, do not understand the difference between ancestral worship and heroic honor. Hence they are controlled and protected by the spirit of the dead.

In order for deliverance ministration to be successful, it is often very important to deal with individual's ancestral background in the spiritual realm, otherwise, the battle of life continues from generation to generation in the form of inheritance and transference of spirits. The following explanations will enable us to differentiate between respect for heroes and worship of ancestors.

Respect for Ancestors

Respect is a type of consideration, admiration or high-level regard given to people for honorable reasons that are worth emulations. There are various reasons for which respect is paid to people after they have passed away from this life. Some of these reasons are cogent and very important to the society, community, institutions and the various groups which they once served or belonged to; or other reasons held important by their family and relations.

Respect for people of great minds and great achievements are enormously honored all over the world. Some of whom became heroes and heroines in life and/or in death such as Martin Luther King (of the African-American race and civil rights initiator); writers and historians (William Shakespeare), artists and actors, inventors, heads of states and presidents (John Fitzgerald Kennedy of USA), kings and queens (like King James of England), princes and princesses, sports men and women, missionaries and evangelists (like David Livingstone, Kathryn Kuhlman, Aimee Semple McPherson), as well as some commoners who have received memorable honors.

The Word of God honors great men and women of faith, who served and pleased God with honesty and sincerity of hearts. Men like Abraham was described as the father of faith and a friend of God; Isaac and Jacob as the great descendants and joint-heirs with Father Abraham **(Hebrews 11: 8-9)**; David as a man after God's own heart who carried the seed of Jesus Christ our Lord. It is pertinent to honor the generals of the Christian faith, because the testimonies of these men and women serve as examples for Christians from generation to generation, till the return of Jesus Christ.

Bartimaeus the blind man, trying to seek attention for the healing of his blind eyes, honored the Lord Jesus Christ by identifying Him thus: "Jesus the Son of David, have mercy on me!" The respect and honor being given to these great men and women of the past is not sinful, and has no demonic connotation, as long as the motive is clear, and there is no hidden agenda. However, if they are worshipped, it then attracts some demonic influences such as will be discussed under Ancestral Worship.

Reference And Research (Library)

While in active journalism, I noticed that one of the hottest news-breaks for media attraction is the death of an important personality. It matters more if that personality belonged to the society in which a particular media operates. When a personality of a high profile—president, prime minister, head of government, head of department, head of institution, political activist, religious leader or VIP—dies, every journalist is put to the task of nosing around and gathering all sorts of information concerning the life history of such a personality.

A media house can endeavor to build a library about the life of a person from the day he was conceived in his mother's womb to the day he departed. If such a person happened to have contributed much to the society or to certain international bodies, then it is obvious that international journalists will follow suit with reports in various international newspapers and magazines. Such personalities make the headlines and make bestsellers for that period in time.

Soon the historical background and achievements of such a one would be noticed in some academic institution's curriculum. Newspaper clippings on such personalities could be found in libraries (national and international). Historians and book writers would also play their part by documenting such information for the benefit of research and posterity. For instance, more often than not, the mention of Martin Luther King often attracts the priority pages of newspapers and magazines around the world. This is because Martin Luther King died as a hero in a good cause, fighting for the right of the black community in American society.

Emulation, Encouragement and Appreciation

Sometimes the lifestyle of people of the past could be a good example for emulation and encouragement to the younger generation. One worthy of such emulation is a young girl, Mary Slessor (*Heroine of Calabar*), the slim Scottish girl who dreamed of being a missionary to Africa at a tender age of about eleven [Basil Miller (1974)].

Mary Slessor's encounter, such as the ability to overcome both the primitive hazards of pioneer mission work and the barbarous social practices of the tribes to whom she was sent; the churches she planted, schools she built, and the children she delivered and the souls saved for the Lord Jesus Christ are all elements of emulation, encouragement and appreciation to serious-minded persons who read about them.

In appreciation of the great works she did in the city of Calabar, in Southern Nigeria, an artist's work reflecting her image is planted for the cynosure of all eyes (if Jesus tarries). The sculpture of Mary Slessor's image erected in a city center is not for worship and idolatry, but for remembrance of courage and good works. An excerpt from her biography reads, *"Remembrance of the young girl who picked up such an undaunted courage for the salvation of souls in the jungle means remembrance of the gospel of our Lord Jesus Christ and the reality of the Cross of Calvary."*

Restoration, Revival And Continuity

It is hoped that one day, a child born to one of the numerous salvages of Mary Slessor will be moved to revive and continue the work that the little missionary established in the one-time jungle of Calabar. Then restoration of the gospel and the lost souls of Calabar will return once again; and Mary Slessor will look down on earth and rejoice with the angels above. Other important reasons for such a revival of her work could be for continuity, encouragement, ideas, studies, remembrance and to update reality.

WORSHIP OF ANCESTORS

If respect for ancestors is that important, why then do some Christians condemn ancestor worship? There is a great difference between respect for ancestors and worship of ancestors. It is very important to differentiate clearly between the two. Respect has been explained above with regard to works, invention and courage that are worthy of emulation and attention of posterity.

Worship of ancestors has to do with idolization of the dead; invocation of the spirit of the dead; seeking protection from the dead; hoping and trusting in the dead; offering prayer to the dead; and visiting the grave of the dead religiously. A dead body is simply dead and is a corpse. Once a dead body enters the grave, its mortal body returns to clay and the soul and spirit of such report back to the Maker, and thereafter are sent to where they belong—Hades (hell) or Paradise (heaven) to await the judgment day.

At this point, the dead is useless. It can neither hear nor see. It no longer belongs to this earth. It is powerless and helpless. It is totally nonexistent. It has no ability whatsoever to pay any form of attention to any caller on earth when it is probably full of regret while waiting to be cast into hell fire.

The graveyard is the habitation of demons and evil spirits. Oftentimes, demons who have no dwelling place seek abode in dead bodies. No normal person dwells in the graveyard except persons involved in occultic practices, such as magicians. Also, individuals possessed by demons who, as a result have lost their mental control, are driven by the demons to dwell among the dead as in the case of the man of Gadarenes.

Mark 5:2, 3 & 15 says,

And when He [Jesus] had come out of the boat, immediately there met Him at the tombs a man with an unclean spirit, who had his dwelling among the tombs, and no one could bind him, not even with chains...

Seeking Guidance and Protection from Ancestors

It is interesting to note that people invoke the spirit of dead ancestors with the intention of seeking protection and guidance for their daily endeavors, especially when a need arises for a family to make a major decision. Some also pour libation to the spirit of dead parents, as a form of worship and adoration. They sing the praise of their dead ones. These form of practices are common in some parts of Africa and Asia.

People who pay devotional attention to the dead are also fond of dedicating newborn babies to ancestral spirits. Ancestral spirits are nothing but demons. Therefore ancestral worship is occultic, so anyone involved in the practice is actually idolizing demons, and honoring the evil works of demons. The demons in charge of a particular ancestral lineage would then put up the body and facial resemblance of the dead members of the family lineage they represent. They will also fake the voices and speak out to the worshippers through various forms of revelations by which they are contacted. The demons will appear anywhere they are called and form a link with other demons in that category according to the order of their operation. In fact a mark of identification is placed on such persons for easy recognition by other demons. Then the demons will begin to act as ancestral gods to the family concerned, and also follow them about.

Once a child is dedicated to ancestral gods, a demon is then assigned to guard and watch over that baby. A mark of identification is also put on that innocent child, which holds him in spiritual bondage. Sometimes the demons possess and control the child and also dwell inside him/her. There are instances, when a child born abroad is dedicated in absentia and it becomes effective through postage of names that are used as point of contact; as soon the names are mentioned and placed on a child through reading of the prayers to the ancestors, the child is immediately possessed by the assigned spirit.

Hence, innocent children suffer from possession of demons of whose existence in their lives they are ignorant. The only clue that a child may have been possessed by an ancestral demon could be traced down to a story told by parents or certain members of their extended family that relates to child dedication. Sometimes the meaning of the names they bear and who gave the name could also give a clue. Sometimes the symptoms the children suffer could reveal ancestral dedication.

INFERTILITY (BARRENNESS)

Infertility is one of the strongest points of contact through which many women are easily lured into the demonic world, and sometimes into occultism. Infertility is the inability to have children. It is a sort of experience that no woman ever wants to go through. It appears in different forms such as: natural abortion or instability of pregnancy, loss of child at birth or just after birth, early age death, inability to become pregnant, absence of fertilization hormone and other problems which could hinder a woman from producing babies.

The Act Of God

Although, there are cases that are meant for the glorification of God's name.. To prove the wonderful working power of God in a miraculous situation, it is pertinent to note that the problems of infertility are not particularly the act of nature; neither are all the doings of God. The case of Father Abraham and Sarah in the book of Genesis is purely an act of God, meant for a purpose. And one of the major purposes was to build the faith of Father Abraham. Father Abraham needed to consolidate his relationship with God by demonstrating a faith which could not be moved or shaken by any situation whatsoever. Father Abraham was expected to exercise the sort of faith that would form the basic part of the inheritance for his joint heir from generation to generation. It must be the faith that could stand the test of time. Accordingly, Father Abraham's faith was tested when he was instructed to give back to God what seemed so precious to him, having waited his whole life for a seed that probably proved his manhood, and finally had a child to inherit him.

Hannah is one of the wonderful women who suffered and overcame infertility after several years of prayer and intercession to God. Her experience and testimony serve as strong encouragement to every woman who has the knowledge of God's Word. Even men and women who do not suffer infertility, are moved to follow the example of Hannah, as a woman who gave back to God that which she wept for—the child Samuel. It is a pleasure of every woman to name her son Samuel; with the intention that the child will dwell in the house of the Lord forever.

The experiences of Sarah and Hannah could be described as a plan purposed by God, as a point of contact to prove the supernatural power of God to everyone who cares to seek Him in spirit and in truth. Sarah and Hannah are the rising hope of all women who believe in God. Many women who have exercised similar faith have a sweet and interesting story to tell the whole world. It is amazing to experience the supernatural touch of God.

The Act of the Enemy

On the other hand, many women suffer infertility as a result of infirmity (sickness and disease). Some others are due to curses—ancestral curse, generational curse or manifestation of direct curse. Some others also suffer infertility as a result of demonic vows sworn or oaths taken by parents or as a sacrifice in place of another thing that was once considered as precious. Others could be the effect of demonic influence. Demonic influence is also a result of incisions made on some parts of the body, consulting satanic agents in search for the cause of problems that might have besieged a person, taking oaths or vows, etc.

These sorts of disturbances push some desperate victims into seeking help wherever it seems possible. During the process of seeking help, many are deceived, and lured into doing things that are scary, dangerous and also foolish. In the process, they have also made vows to demons and fetish priests. Some women seeking fertility of the womb have had cause to drink and swallow all sorts of mixed concoctions. Some have had cause to sleep at riverbanks in the middle of the nights; some have been bathed with concoctions and also initiated into the demonic world.

As a result of consultations made through palm reading, stargazing, mediums, divination and other forms of spiritism, children born to the victims of the demonic world, also suffer from all sorts of demonic oppression and frustration. Some of the demonic forces that affect such children also link them up with similar demonic contamination. Hence, parents transfer the act of clairvoyance to their wards that also fall prey to demonic consultation.

Most likely the fundamental link at the point of pregnancy and during the embryonic age often gives them up to such spirits as the mermaid spirit, water spirit and serpentine spirit (snake spirit). Note that infertility applies to both the male and the female sex. It seems to be more pronounced with the women because they bear the obvious side of the burden, as they have to carry the pregnancy to the glaring of all eyes. The men's burden is hidden, yet it could be worse. Some women are paid and pampered to keep the secret of the men's infertility, while they seek pregnancy from elsewhere. Unfortunately, some husbands of women victimized by infertility sometimes seek refuge in glorified adultery (polygamy).

Contamination by Birth

An involvement of a parent in clairvoyance, seeking consultation from agents of Satan, brings an automatic contamination to a child born into that family. If such a child one day decides to surrender himself to the Lordship of Jesus Christ, there will be a need for such a child to also renounce any form of association with the demonic world. Sometimes one may not be aware of such an act having taken place. In view of such ignorance, it is ideal for one to investigate his or her childhood experiences.

On the other hand, one is able to trace contamination through the kind of dreams that one often has; through behaviors, attitude and characteristics that one often displays; through the types of relationships that one often experiences with both same and opposite sexes; through some consistent seasonal encounters; through sicknesses, diseases and other attacks from which one suffers; and also through family history (some strange occurrences that could be consistent among family members and relations).

To be on the safe side, it is better to seek a deliverance checkup as one seeks a medical checkup to ensure that one has a free spirit and free soul to worship God in spirit and in truth. Otherwise, if there is any such contamination in one's life, no matter how active one could be in the things of God, one may be experiencing some sort of hindrances. Such hindrance may be loss of property; financial lack or mismanagement; lack of ability to excel despite academic or professional qualification; lack of opportunity in one's general life; consistent occurrence of disaster; general failure; disappointments; rejection; sorrow; suppression, frustration, depression; and also lack of joy and peace of mind.

When the negative part of one's life outweighs the positive achievements, there is need for a spiritual checkup. When disaster often occurs shortly after or in the midst of success, there is need for spiritual checkup. When there is frustration, suppression or depression at the end of the day or at short interval despite bright achievements, there is need for a spiritual checkup. When there is often an accusation even when it is not necessary, there is need for a spiritual checkup. When all efforts to block a loophole seem hopeless, then there is need for a spiritual checkup.

Don't wait until it is too late, and do not feel too big or too important to seek a deliverance checkup; everyone is equal before the enemy, the destroyer of the human body. If it is not a shame to seek a medical checkup in the hospital, where the medical personnel could be involved in some sort of occultism, as told by Rebecca Brown in her book "*He Came to Set the Captive Free* (1992)," then it is rather a great blessing to seek a deliverance checkup in the presence of the Lord God of Hosts.

Contamination by Marriage

Although the Word of God states that God ordains marriage, many people do not allow God to participate in their marriage procedure and bless it. They prefer to seek knowledge of a suitor through consultation with mediums, sorcerers, witchdoctors, palmists and other occultic means. Unknown to the seekers, this type of consultation opens up a marriage to demonic interferences. Later on, such a marriage can be haunted by the demons that were consulted. There are cases when individuals lure suitors by casting spells of "love." Any marriage that is built on demonic or occultic devices is bound to attract some sort of repercussion in the life of the individual involved, and also affect the innocent individual who fell victim to it. Deception and lies don't last very long; no matter how one tries to endure a spellbound marriage, it is advisable to seek a deliverance checkup to break the uncomfortable interferences that may be clouding the home.

Similarly, persons contaminated by birth do have a carry-over into their marriage life. There are cases where oaths were taken to dedicate a child to a demonic spirit that was consulted during the period of infertility. Such vows could hinder one from marriage. Where marriage occurs, such marriages are bedeviled with strange problems; some of which may result in broken homes, separation, divorce, adultery and unnecessary interferences. Covenants and vows made could cause infertility or constant loss of pregnancy and problems with childbirth.

There are cases, where the demon concerned plays the role of a spirit husband or wife to victims. The spirit partner either drives away intending suitors, or sends away any spouse with whom one settles down. That is why some individuals end up marrying two to five times. Often times when such a situation arises, there is a vow or oath or covenant involved, which must be broken. Otherwise, a person will think God is yet to hear his or her cry.

The answer to your problem is the need for investigation, counsel, and deliverance ministration. Some other times, the person with whom one gets involved could bring contamination into one's life and marriage. It is a simple analogy that if you drink from a dirty cup, particles from the dirty cup will go inside your body and contaminate your body. Unless you flush out the dirt, you will remain contaminated and this could be dangerous to your health.

SALVATION

The Scriptures say, "Work out your own salvation with fear and trembling" (**Philippians 2:12**). This means that after one has made a decision to accept Christ, one has to begin a schedule of gradual growth, centered on sanctification and purification, which is not a one-day affair. It is a lifetime affair.

The first decision made is a sort of admission into the Christian race. There is a time of listening to lectures, a time of assignment and homework; a time of class tests, to be tried and tempted; a time of examination and promotion and so on and on it goes; from milk feeding to spoon feeding and then to chewing and cracking ... The Christian life is a process. If one does not make an effort to grow, one will remain a baby, and later this could result in being crippled or being a burden to others. Refusal to learn causes failure.

Laziness has no place in the kingdom of God. People who are lazy must be rebuked and scolded to sit up; otherwise, such persons will be a disgrace to the body of Christ. No parent can tolerate a baby who refuses to grow. An effort will be made to consult medical personnel and specialists to diagnose the problem until a solution is discovered. The medical personnel involved go into a period of research to investigate the root cause of the prevailing problem that is hindering the growth of a child.

Similarly, Christians need to make research, read and study the situation surrounding their lives, so that success and victory could be celebrated to the glorification of God's name. Do not depend on your personal feeling and what you think is comfortable and suitable for you. Wake up to responsibility, and conquer the marital problems in your family. Investigate the root cause of the problem interfering with you rather than blaming your spouse for all the short-comings. In fact, it could be an ancestral curse from your family background. It could be a curse placed on you or a witchcraft spell cast on you. Do not allow the enemy to scatter your home. Your daily song of victory should be "Till death do us part."

DIVORCE AND SEPARATION

People make mistakes when they are desperately in love or under infatuation. People in love do not usually take counsel or listen to any form of advice that cautions their decision to marry without investigating an intended spouse. Deficient approach to marital relationship has opened the door of the Christian community to interfering spirits that are tearing homes apart.

Sometimes, ministers have no choice but to approve separation for couples to attend counseling sessions and deliverance ministration to sort out their differences. In certain cases, the final decision may be divorce if the parties concerned are not showing any sense of responsibility toward each other. However, many couples attending counseling sessions have confessed that if they have had knowledge of deliverance ministration, they would have restored their former relationships rather than divorced.

In recent times, many people who claim to be Christians, including "supposed" ministers of the gospel, separate or divorce their spouses over trivial matters that could be dealt with through deliverance ministration. They even go to the law court to seek divorce so they can remarry. Oh what a shame to hear of such negatives. They don't believe in deliverance ministration, but they believe in manmade laws that are instituted for the courts.

What kind of gospel do such persons preach; what is the foundation of their faith? Are you aware that there are demons and principalities of darkness that control marriages and broken homes? Do you know that marriage is a holy institution ordained by God, and it is the first institution that God set up? That is why the enemy is fighting homes and separating flesh from bones, so that he can win more followers to accompany him to hell.

Unfortunately, when parents divorce, the children suffer the consequences of hurts. In some cases, the spirit of divorce creates a new leaf of curses on innocent children. Any acclaimed Christian contemplating separation or divorce must carefully consider the repercussion on the offspring of the marriage.

Like any other sin, divorce has serious consequences leading to hell. It is not enough to call it quits, but to seriously consider reconciliation. How about that? Food for thought! Truth is bitter, and hard to swallow. Isn't it? Of course, it is.

How A Christian Is Affected By Demonic Spirits

- Involuntary participation.
- Unwillingness to accept and cooperate with deliverance
- Lack of submissiveness to biblical truth
- Exhibition of pride and ego
- Entertaining a religious spirit
- Refusal to break demonic attachment to family, ancestors, and reincarnation.

Poetic Expression Three

WAR AGAINST DISOBEDIENCE

War against disobedience
It is time to war against disobedience
Disobedience is pride
I shall humble myself
Disobedience is destruction
I shall not perish
I shall war against disobedience

War against disobedience
It is time to war against disobedience
Disobedience is rude
I shall respect correction
Disobedience is ignorance
I shall be studious
I shall war against disobedience

War against disobedience
Come let us rise against disobedience
Disobedience is an evil spirit
It is an agent of Satan
I shall not permit it
It destroys peace
I shall war against disobedience

War against disobedience
I have conquered disobedience
It shall no longer come nigh
I have overcome disobedience
It shall no longer tempt me
I have possessed my authority

The Lord has won the battle for me
And disobedience has disappeared.

Pauline Walley, November 1996

Chapter Three

THE REASONS FOR DELIVERANCE

After the deception of Satan had caused the fall of Adam and Eve, the next sin recorded in the Holy Scripture was the killing of Abel by his brother Cain. Before the murder of Abel, Cain had displayed the spirit of anger in the highest order, which motivated killing. Cain did not only murder his brother Abel, but he was also dishonest. He lied when God enquired of the whereabouts of his brother, saying, "I do not know." Again Cain was rude to God, asking, "Am I my brother's keeper?" **(Genesis 4:1-10)**

There and then, Cain was cursed and man was cursed; because the curse that came upon him affected all men, just like the curse placed upon his parents Adam and Eve had affected him, and all the generations that followed till this day. While the initial sin of disobedience against the Word of God attracted the need for redemption which God promised **(Genesis 3:15)**, the curse placed on man also attracted deliverance: "**...And the Lord set a mark on Cain, lest anyone finding him should kill him**" **(Genesis 4:15)**.

There is a need for deliverance ministration after one has responded to a gospel message. Deliverance ministration is a follow-up session that keeps one closer to identifying with Christ Jesus. Deliverance is a process of separating and cleansing oneself from the old ways in order to receive renewal of spirit, soul and body. The process of deliverance enables one to make conscious effort to renew one's character, behavior and attitude to conform to the image and likeness of God. It is a conscious effort that one makes to renounce a former relationship with evil and confess a new relationship with Christ Jesus.

Some people have the tendency of conforming with evil even after they have gone to church. There are churchgoers who indulge in occultic practices because of their background. Such individuals need deliverance ministration in order to stabilize their relationship with Christ Jesus; otherwise, their past behavior will be interfering with their Christian lifestyle. Many people have unconfessed sin that they assume does not need to be mentioned; meanwhile, that sin has a stronghold on their life. That sin has become a loophole for certain atrocities committed unconsciously and unwillingly.

Cain: Some churchgoers assume God does not care about their weaknesses or temperaments because they exhibit some revelatory gifts like visions and dreams, and also claim that they hear the voice of God. Cain also heard the voice of God. He had a conversation with God, yet he ignored God's warning and went ahead to kill his brother Cain because he refused to control his anger (**Genesis 4:1-15**).

In recent times, many people exhibit anger and hatred within and around church auditoriums and premises. Because of the lack of the fear of God, these individuals have no conscience when they are in the presence of the Most Holy One. They make outrageous utterances and demonstrate behaviors that are not far from being satanic. There are cases when people who are expected to be church leaders despise the presence of God, even before unbelievers and new converts while prayer and fasting are in session. Whatever influences the works of the flesh while we are still in the house of the Lord need to be cast out.

Abraham: Abraham was in the presence of God offering sacrifices after a brief conversation, when an evil spirit emerged in form of vultures to interfere with him. A vulture represents the spirit of the graveyard. The devil had come to steal away the promises that God was investing into Abraham. **"And when the vultures came down on the carcasses, Abram drove them away" (Genesis 15:11).** By driving away the vultures, Abraham was performing the act of deliverance ministration upon himself.

Jesus said when an unclean spirit goes out of a man, he goes out wandering and seeking another place to inhabit; if he finds no resting place, he returns with seven stronger spirits that are more wicked than himself (**Matthew 12:43-45**). After the vultures had been driven away, the enemy took another form and appeared again while Abraham was still in the presence of God. **"...a deep sleep fell upon Abram; and behold, horror and great darkness fell upon him" Genesis 15:12).** The horror and great darkness symbolize the 400 years of affliction that came upon the descendants of Abraham in Egypt.

THE DESCENDANTS OF ABRAHAM

When God was taking the descendants of Abraham to the Promised Land, He gave them the Ten Commandments, with statutes and laws that would enable them to keep a holy relationship with Him. The Israelites where instructed to abstain from any type of relationship that would corrupt the image and likeness of God in them and their posterity. All communion with the nations around them was forbidden because of the tendency of mingling with idolatry.

Deuteronomy 7:1-8 (KJV) says,

When the LORD thy God shall bring thee into the land whither thou goest to possess it, and hath cast out many nations before thee, the Hittites, and the Girgashites, and the Amorites, and the Canaanites, and the Perizzites, and the Hivites, and the Jebusites, seven nations greater and mightier than thou;

And when the LORD thy God shall deliver them before thee; <u>thou shalt smite them, and utterly destroy them; thou shalt make no covenant with them, nor shew mercy unto them;</u>

<u>Neither shalt thou make marriages with them</u>; thy daughter thou shalt not give unto his son, nor his daughter shalt thou take unto thy son.

<u>For they will turn away thy son from following me, that they may serve other gods</u>; so will the anger of the LORD be kindled against you, and destroy thee suddenly.

But thus shall ye deal with them; ye shall destroy their altars, and break down their images, and cut down their groves, and burn their graven images with fire.

For thou art an holy people unto the LORD thy God; the LORD thy God hath chosen thee to be a special people unto himself, above all people that are upon the face of the earth.

The LORD did not set his love upon you, nor choose you, because ye were more

in number than any people; for ye were the fewest of all people;
    But because the LORD loved you, and because he would keep the oath which he had sworn unto your fathers, hath the LORD brought you out with a mighty hand, and redeemed you out of the house of bondmen, from the hand of Pharaoh king of Egypt. [*Underlining by author.*]

THE KINGS' RESPONSE TO DELIVERANCE

The reality of the need for deliverance was evident in the lives of King David's descendants, as most of them could not abide by the commandments and statutes that were handed over to them. Some of the kings of Israel reverenced God and sought help from the priests and prophets of their days. Some lacked the fear of God, and did not heed the warnings that came through the priests and prophets. Solomon started well immediately after he assumed the throne, but he could not maintain his relationship with the Almighty God.

When King Solomon rose to fame, he transgressed the law of God and compromised the glory of God for his self-centered ambition. Some of the sins committed by King Solomon became a generational stronghold among his descendants. The sins also attracted curses, as Satan capitalized on them, and held innocent children in bondage. Hence there was continuous transgression of the law of God.

1 Kings 11:1-3 states,

But King Solomon loved many foreign women, as well as the daughter of Pharaoh;

women of the Moabites, Ammonites, Edomites, Sidonians, and Hittites- from the nations of whom the Lord had said to the children of Israel, " You shall not intermarry with them, or they with you. <u>For surely they will turn away your hearts after their gods.</u>" <u>Solomon clung to these in love.</u> And he had seven hundred wives, princesses, and three hundred concubines; and his wives turned away his heart. [*Underlining by author.*]

KING SOLOMON'S FIRST DISOBEDIENCE

Solomon transgressed the law that forbade intermarriage between the children of Israel and some specific nations that had been named in **Deuteronomy 7:1** (the Moabites, Ammonites, Edomites, Sidonians, and the Hittites); because they (the nations in question) lacked the fear of the Almighty God, the Maker of mankind. Solomon was aware of the fact that intermarriage with the nations noted would cause the children of Israel much harm. He was aware that such marriage alliances would bring about the impartation of sin and the immoral behavior prevalent in those nations, all of which were displeasing to God. He was aware that women from the corrupted nations would not compromise the worship of the gods of their fathers. That marriage to a woman from any of these nations meant a marriage to their idols.

Solomon's marriage to the women from idolatrous nations opened the door to demonic activities that infiltrated the nation of Israel, and defiled the children of the Most High God. King Solomon, a dedicated man of God, to whom God had revealed Himself, and covenanted an allegiance, later defected. His alliance and association with foreign kingdoms lured him into sin. He was offered beautiful women with demonic spirits, demonic characters and demonic worship. The spirit of lust in the highest order of principalities and powers of darkness attacked and polluted his heart.

The possession of these women meant the possession of demonic properties, which paved the way for Satan to have free access to claim legal domination in the family of Solomon. Of course, both the nation of Israel and members of his family suffered for this sin of disobedience.

Application

In modern times, dedicated Christians are advised to avoid intermarriage with persons who do not belong to the Christian faith. A marriage to an unbeliever is like a marriage to a prospective agent of Satan. This sort of marriage can (sometimes, not in all cases) be an importation of demons into the body and the home. That is why we are warned with the words **"...do not be unequally yoked with an unbeliever" (2 Corinthians 6:14).** Where the couple are of different spiritual beliefs, there is likely to be a disagreement. Disagreement will generate disunity, unhappiness and misunderstanding, which could lead to hatred and marital breakdown. It takes the intervention of God to have an unbelieving spouse surrender his or her life to the Lord Jesus Christ, especially in cases where the unbelieving partner is involved in the worship of idol or occult.

1 Corinthians 6:15-17 states,

Do you not know that your bodies are members of Christ? Shall I then take the members of Christ and make them members of a harlot? Certainly not! Or

75

> do you not know that he who is joined to a harlot is one body with her? For "The two," He says, "shall become one flesh." But he who is joined to the Lord is one spirit with Him.

KING SOLOMON'S SECOND DISOBEDIENCE

It is recorded in 1 Kings 11:4-6 that,

> For it was so, when Solomon was old that his wives turned his heart after other gods; and his heart was not loyal to the Lord his God, as was the heart of his father David. For Solomon went after Ashtoreth the goddess of the Sidonians, and after Milcom the abomination of the Ammonites. Solomon did evil in the sight of the Lord, and did not fully follow the Lord, as did his father David.

Application

Declaration of love to a woman means surrendering oneself to her totally, as the two—man and woman—have become one flesh, one body in spirit and soul; for as the Scripture states "... a man shall be joined to his wife, and the two shall become one flesh..." and "... whatsoever God has joined together, let no man put asunder." God has spoken from creation, and His Word cannot return unto Him without accomplishing (fulfilling) the purpose for which it has been sent forth. By this Word of God, King Solomon was bound to satisfy his foreign wives, in order to achieve a successful marriage. His heart became corrupted because he was not able to convert those ladies to worship his Holy God. The demons of religion and deception captured his godly abilities.

The God-fearing desires that had brought wealth and fame to him had been corrupted by the women with whom he later shared his love, his body, his heart, and everything he had. Since the act of sexuality (intercourse) is a powerful means of unity in marriage, King Solomon's heart became knitted with the devilish spirits that were in possession of those foreign women.

In recent times, many Christians have fallen prey to men and women who are looking for faithful spouses to marry. These rich individuals often present themselves as harmless and conform to the principles of the "don't touch" before marriage. Some men will make promises not to interfere with the ladies' church activities so long as they (the men) are not pestered to become involved. Based on this agreement, the men will pretentiously participate actively in all church activities. They will even try to befriend the ministers in charge just to ensure that the intended marriage is accepted. Immediately after marriage the man declares his stand, and the woman is forced to live a life of compromise. There are cases where the men or women concerned have later confessed to be agents of Satan, or members of occult groups.

Unfortunately, the Christian partners involved have been warned and threatened never to mention it, else they will face the consequences. In order to maintain their relationship with God, the Christian spouses in such relationships have sought the assistance of ministers, whose prayers have been helpful. In some cases the Christian partner who could not resist the devil often backslide, or become lukewarm.

KING SOLOMON'S THIRD DISOBEDIENCE

Then Solomon built a high place for Chemosh, the abomination of Moab, on the hill that is east of Jerusalem, and for Molech the abomination of the people of Ammon. And he did likewise for all his foreign wives, who burned incense and sacrificed to their gods **(1 Kings 11:7-8)**. Having been proclaimed a great king whose wealth had no comparison in the whole world, either in measure of wisdom, material possession, or any such prosperity as one could ever think of, King Solomon had no choice but to meet up with the responsibilities that would reflect such greatness in his marriage. Unfortunately, Solomon built temples for the gods that the women he married served in order to fulfill his alliance with the nations that the women came from.

In this case, he compromised his allegiance to God for the worship of foreign idols. He built temples for the idols and encouraged the worship of foreign gods, which was an abomination to the Most Holy God. Some Christians who have gone into marriages with people of different faith and belief have ended up compromising their salvation, for the sake of peace in the home. While such a compromise is the act of submission to one's spouse, it is an act of disobedience to God.

The Repercussion of Solomon's Disobedience

The Lord became angry with Solomon, because his heart had turned from the Lord God of Israel, who had appeared to him twice, and had commanded him concerning this thing, that he should not go after other gods; but Solomon did not keep what the Lord had commanded. Therefore the Lord said to Solomon, **"Because you have done this, and have not kept My covenant and My statutes, which I have** commanded you, I will surely tear the kingdom away from you and give it to your servant" (1 Kings 11:9-11).

Disobedience to the Word of God could be terrible, especially in the case where a person had tasted and seen the glory of God. Samuel the prophet told King Saul that, **"The act of disobedience is like the sin of witchcraft."** The book of Revelation says **"...You are neither hot nor cold, I will spew you out of my mouth"** (Revelation 3:16).

Application

Many times we have heard news of shame and disgrace coming upon Christian brethren who have been known for reputable standing, and we wonder why God allowed such a thing to happen. Sometimes disgraceful acts of some personalities have been handled diplomatically and the brethren concerned are restored to position peacefully because they showed remorse when they were found out. In some cases, persons involved defected completely from the Christian faith or migrated to another city to seek refuge.

In other cases, it has been noticed that when some "great" ministers of the faith passed away, members of their family lost hold of continuity. It is because the kingdom has been torn away without notice of the fellowship concerned. Where the gifts of revelation are not suppressed, some of these issues are revealed, discussed and order is restored for the sake of the advancement of the gospel of our Lord Jesus Christ.

HEREDITY (TRANSFERENCE OF SIN)

1 Kings 11:12, 13 states,

Nevertheless I will not do it in your days, for the sake of your father David; but I will tear it out of the hand of your son. However I will not tear away the whole kingdom, but I will give one tribe to your son for the sake of my servant David, and for the sake of Jerusalem which I have chosen.

The repercussion of King Solomon's sin became an inheritance that passed on from generation to generation. Rehoboam, having witnessed both the glory of God and the abomination of his father with the foreign wives, presented himself as a rough and wicked king. His words had no moral touch from the laws of God. Rehoboam's disrespectful character encouraged the division of the kingdom into two – the Northern Kingdom being Israel and the Southern Kingdom being Judah.

The children of Israel became enemies to themselves, and the worship of foreign gods surged higher than ever. The Northern Kingdom defected completely from worshiping the Most High God while the descendants of David, after Solomon's generation, struggled to abide in the fear of the Most High God as the demonic spirit of religion had infiltrated their home.

Deliverance Ignored

It is obviously noted that Solomon ignored the need for deliverance even after he had been notified of his errors. He made little effort to rectify his mistakes, so there was no room for repentance or deliverance. Unlike his father David who was quick to make repentance, Solomon was probably too proud to rectify his errors and renew his allegiance with God. This error cost him the whole land of Israel.

The Need for Deliverance

Several decades after the death of King Solomon, the first ten sets of kings that inherited the throne of the Southern kingdom either encouraged idolatry or warred against it. In fact, all of them, with the exception of about five who conducted deliverance for the whole nation, actually did evil in the sight of God. There were some who returned to God, yet because they had initially entangled themselves with immorality and idolatry, and had not sought for deliverance from those demonic alliance, their hearts were still not pure, so they backslid.

FIRST GENERATION OF SOLOMON – REHOBOAM
Rehobaom Rejected Deliverance

1 Kings 14:21-24,

And Rehoboam the son of Solomon reigned in Judah. Rehoboam was forty-one years old when he became king. He reigned seventeen years in Jerusalem, the city that the Lord had chosen out of all the tribes of Israel, to put His name there. His mother's name was Naamah, an Ammonitess. Now Judah did evil in the sight of the Lord, and they provoked Him to jealousy with their sins which they committed, more than all

that their fathers had done. For they also built for themselves high places, sacred pillars, and wooden images on every high hill and under every green tree. And there were also perverted persons in the land. They did according to all the abominations of the nations which the Lord had cast out before the children of Israel. [*Underlining by author.*]

Here, it is clear that his mother, an Ammonitess, who was one of the foreign wives of King Solomon, had brought up Rehoboam. Apparently, Rehoboam had been dedicated to the demonic gods of Ammon, and had been involved in sacrifices and burning of incense to foreign gods even before he inherited the throne.

With the encouragement of his Ammonitess mother, Rehoboam of course showered the idolized temples with all the great wealth of the kingdom, and this provoked God to jealousy. This sort of sin needs the intervention of deliverance ministration to purify and sanctify Rehoboam. An ordinary prayer of confession is not enough to set him free. All the demons that abode in him needed to be rebuked and cast out of his spirit, soul, and body. The presence of evil in his life corrupted his lifestyle, because his heart, which was supposed to be the temple of the living God, had become an abode for evil spirits. Rohoboam was therefore influenced by evil spirits and did not pay attention to the Most Holy One.

SECOND GENERATION OF SOLOMON – ABIJAM
Abijam Rejected Deliverance

After the death of Rehoboam, Abijam his son inherited the throne. Abijam was described as a man who walked in all the sins of his father. That means Abijam inherited all kinds of evil that his father ever practiced, and was probably very obnoxious. He had no fear of God and did evil according to the dictation of the demons that possessed him.

1 Kings 15:1-5 records,

> **...Abijam became king over Judah...And he walked in all the sins of his father, which he had done before him; his heart was not loyal to the Lord his God, as was the heart of his father David. Nevertheless for David's sake the Lord his God gave him a lamp in Jerusalem, by setting up his son after him and by establishing Jerusalem; because David did what was right in the eyes of the Lord, and had not turned aside from anything that He commanded him all the days of his life, except in the matter of Uriah the Hittite.**

King Abijam was another serious case for deliverance. It is obvious that like father, like son. Children learn by sight, and usually copy whatever they see their parents do. Abijam followed his father, Rehoboam's footsteps. His three-year reign was evil-oriented. There was no record that Abijam sought help from either the priests or the prophets of his days.

THIRD GENERATION OF SOLOMON – ASA
Asa Accepted Deliverance

Despite the intensity of evil that Asa witnessed in his household, Asa distinguished his ways and lifestyle from that of his family. He separated himself and accomplished a unique name that conformed to the Davidic covenant. He took a charismatic approach to eradicate the practice of evil starting from his home. He removed his grandmother from being queen so that he could function effectively as a man that fears the Lord.

1 Kings 15:9-15 states,

In the twentieth year of Jeroboam king of Israel, Asa became king over Judah. And he reigned forty-one years in Jerusalem. His grandmother's name was Maachah, the granddaughter of Abishalom. Asa did what was right in the eyes of the Lord, as did his father David. <u>And he banished the perverted persons from the land, and removed all the idols that his fathers had made.</u> Also <u>he moved Maachah his grandmother from being queen mother, because she had made an obscene image of Ashterah.</u> And <u>Asa cut down her obscene image and burned it</u> by the Brook Kidron. But the high places were not removed. Nevertheless Asa's heart was loyal to the Lord all his days. He also brought into the house of the Lord the things that his father had dedicated, and the things that he himself had dedicated: silver and gold and utensils. [*Underlining by author.*]

King David was a man who honored the ministers of God - prophets and priests. He was conscious of the constant need for deliverance ministration—which is the same as purification and sanctification. Every now and then, David accepted his errors and called for the ministers of God to lead him into a period of cleansing (**Psalm 51**).

Like his great-grandfather David, King Asa accepted the

idea of deliverance ministration. He took a bold decision to cleanse himself and the kingdom of all the demonic activities that had infiltrated the throne and the house of David. Asa was bold enough to do away with his own grandmother, along with the immoral persons in the land. Here, it is clear that the Priest or Prophet in charge of the Temple of Judah at that period believed in deliverance ministration, and also encouraged it. The priest gave King Asa counsel and the necessary spiritual support to do what was right in the sight of the Lord.

In recent times, many ministers of God have not been bold enough to take stringent steps to correct misbehaviors among members of their own families. There has been a lot of compromise, because of fear of persecution.

FOURTH GENERATION OF SOLOMON – JEHOSHAPHAT
Jehoshaphat Accepted Deliverance

Jehoshaphat is the first king that took directly after his immediate father Asa by demonstrating the fear of God since the generation of David and Solomon. Like his father Asa, Jehoshaphat also eliminated evils from the land and maintained a sense of revival that kept the people closer to God.

1 Kings 22:41-50 says,

Jehoshaphat the son of Asa...was thirty-five years old when he became king, and he reigned twenty-five years in Jerusalem... And he walked in all the ways of his father Asa. He did not turn aside from them, doing what was right in the eyes of the Lord. Nevertheless the high places were not taken away, for the people offered

sacrifices and burned incense on the high places. Also Jehoshaphat made peace with the king of Israel…And <u>the rest of the perverted persons who remained in the days of his father Asa, he banished from the land.</u> [*Underlining by author.*]

During the forty-one years of the reign of his father Asa, Jehoshaphat had watched and followed the ways of his father. He had been brought up to walk in the fear of the Lord God Most Holy. He also inherited the love of God, and was loyal to the Lord. In fact, he sought the face of God, and inquired of Him in most of the decisions he took for the kingdom. He was the first king to make peace with the Northern Kingdom since the division. Unfortunately, King Ahab took advantage of the peace treaty and manipulated him to join him at war against Syria with King Ahab of Israel in the Northern Kingdom caused his downfall.

FIFTH GENERATION OF SOLOMON – JEHORAM
Jehoram Rejected Deliverance

2 Kings 8:16-24 says,

…Jehoram the son of Jehoshaphat began to reign as king of Judah. He was thirty-two years old when he became king, and he reigned eight years in Jerusalem. And he walked in the ways of the kings of Israel, just as the house of Ahab had done, <u>for the daughter of Ahab was his wife, and he did evil in the sight of the Lord</u>. Yet the Lord would not destroy Judah, for the sake of his servant David, as He promised

him to give a lamp to him and his sons forever... [*Underlining by author.*]

Although Jehoshaphat loved the Lord and was loyal, he probably did not inquire about the peace treaty signed with his brethren in the Northern Kingdom of Israel. His son Jehoram took advantage of that alliance and married Ahab's daughter. Unfortunately, Ahab's wife Jezeebel was an idolatress, Baal worshipper. Once again, intermarriage brought woe upon the house of David in the Southern Kingdom of Judah. Jehoram, like Solomon his great-grandfather, lived in sin, and did not recognize the presence of the Lord. He did not repent, neither did he seek deliverance for the nation.

SIXTH GENERATION OF SOLOMON – AHAZIAH
Ahaziah Rejected Deliverance

2 Kings 8:25-27 says,

...Ahaziah the son of Jehoram King of Judah began to reign. Ahaziah was twenty-two years old when he became king, and he reigned one year in Jerusalem. His mother's name was Athaliah the granddaughter of Omri, king of Israel. And he walked in the ways of the house of Ahab, and did evil in the sight of the Lord as the house of Ahab had done, for he was the son-in-law of the house of Ahab.
[*Underlining by author.*]

Once again, the backslidden spirit (demon) was thriving among the children of Judah. The peace treaty with the ungodly was causing great harm. The marriage to ungodly women who had no respect for the Lord Most Holy had given room to demons, powers and principalities of darkness to gain legal operation in the house of David. Once more, God was provoked to jealousy as He watched the children of Judah splash His "blessed" wealth on idols.

SEVENTH GENERATION OF SOLOMON – JOASH
Joash Accepted Deliverance

2 Chronicles 22:10-12 says,

Now when Athaliah the mother of Ahaziah saw that her son was dead, she arose and destroyed all the royal heirs of the house of Judah. But Jehoshabeath, the daughter of the king, took Joash the son of Ahaziah, and stole him away from among the king's sons who were being murdered, and put him and his nurse in a bedroom. So Jehoshabeath, the daughter of King Jehoram the wife of Jehoida the priest (for she was the sister of Ahaziah), hid him from Athaliah so that she did not kill him. And he was hidden with them in the house of God for six years, while Athaliah reigned over the land.

2 Kings 12:1-3 says,

In the seventh year of Jehu, Joash became king, and he reigned forty years in Jerusalem. His mother's name was Zibiah of Beersheba. Joash did what was right in the sight of the Lord all the days in which Jehoida the priest instructed him. But the high places were not taken away; the

people still sacrificed and burned incense on the high places. [*Underlining by author.*]

The reign of Joash witnessed a great revival with the support of a God-fearing man called Jehoiada. Joash had been raised by an aunt who was married to a man of God, Jehoiada. Jehoiada was determined to revive the people of God. He instructed the boy Joash in the way of the Lord. As long as Priest Jehoiada was alive, the children of Judah and the young king acknowledged the presence of the Most Holy One.

Deliverance was conducted throughout the land of Judah. The temples of Baal were torn down and the altars and images were destroyed while the priest of Baal was killed. The house of the Lord was refurbished. The laws of God were quickened into the life of the people. A proclamation was made throughout Judah and Jerusalem to impose the commandments and statutes that God gave to Moses regarding the land of Israel. The worship services in the house of the Lord were resuscitated. The ministers of God were also restored to duty, and given their due recognition. Hence the people returned to the Lord their God.

Backslidden Spirit

However, after the death of the Priest Jehoiada, some of the men who ignored the deliverance ministration conducted, lured the young king into sin. This happened because a total deliverance was not actually conducted. The high places built by King Solomon for his foreign wives were not destroyed. This gave room for the demons to activate themselves and attack the younger generation. Hence the worship of wooden images and Baal was revoked in the land of Judah while the young King Joash was still on the throne.

Despite incessant warnings by the prophets of God, King Joash continued in sin. He ignored the importance of the deliverance he had enjoyed in the beginning. He rejected the need for repentance. Rather, he persecuted and killed the prophets of God—Zachariah, the son of the Priest who saved his life. This caused another setback for the house of Judah.

Joash's failure had a strong link to the demon of backsliding that had penetrated the family since the time of Solomon. Hence the backslidden spirit had been passed on through ancestral transference. Joash failed because he was still very young when he assumed the throne. Although he was reigning as king, he did not make the decision for divine restoration. He was instructed as a child and he obediently cooperated with his counselors.

When Joash matured in age, he had the opportunity to relate with his peers and the people of his generation. At this point he probably ignored the counsel of the elders and went his own way to mingle with idolatry.

EIGHTH GENERATION OF SOLOMON - AMAZIAH
<u>Deliverance Accepted But Ignored</u>

2 Kings 14:1-4,

...Amaziah the son of Joash, king of Judah, became king. He was twenty-five years old when he became king, and he reigned twenty-nine years in Jerusalem. His mother's name was Jehoaddan of Jerusalem. And he did what was right in the sight of the Lord, yet not like his father David; he did everything as his father Joash had done. However, the high places were not taken away, and the

people still sacrificed and burned incense on the high places. Now it happened, as soon as the kingdom was established in his hand, that he executed his servants who had murdered his father the king.

Amaziah, having witnessed the tragic end of his father who had a successful reign in the beginning, initially decided to please God. As usual, he accepted the purification and sanctification sermon of the priest, and encouraged his people to follow suit. But, like his father, he cherished the invocation of his foreign ancestral worship. The high places were not destroyed; so the principalities of darkness that controlled those high places were able to reinforce their attack on the children of Judah. Like his father Joash and ancestor king Solomon, Amaziah did not repent. Neither did he recognize the voice of the prophets of the Lord. He ended his life in a sad way.

NINTH GENERATION OF SOLOMON – AZARIAH
Deliverance Accepted But Ignored

2 Kings 15:1-5,

...Azariah the son of Amaziah king of Judah, became king. He was sixteen years old when he became king, and he reigned fifty-two years in Jerusalem. His mother's name was Jecholiah of Jerusalem. And he did what was right in the sight of the Lord, according to all that his father Amaziah had done, except that the high places were not removed; the people still sacrificed and burned incense on the high places. Then the Lord struck the king, so that he was a

leper until the day of his death; so he dwelt in an isolated house. And Jotham the king's son was over the royal house, judging the people of the land.

The high places persistently became a snare to the kings of Judah. The principalities and powers that dwelt in the high places deprived them of enjoying their blessings. The spirit of idolatry arrested their attention and clouded their vision. Azariah tried his best to serve the Lord; but the principalities fought against his interest. His memory was captured, and he soon forgot that the priest in the house of the Lord could minister deliverance to his soul. Even when he was smitten with leprosy, he could not gather himself to accept the law of cleansing and purification in the Law of Moses.

TENTH GENERATION OF SOLOMON - JOTHAM
Deliverance Accepted and Observed

2 Kings 15:32-35 says,

...Jotham the son of Uzziah, king of Judah, began to reign. He was twenty-five years old when he became king, and he reigned sixteen years in Jerusalem. His mother's name was Jerusha the daughter of Zadok. (Zadok the priest) And he did what was right in the sight of the Lord; he did according to all that the father Uzziah had done. However the high places were not removed; the people still sacrificed and burned incense on the high places. He built the upper gate of the house of the Lord.

Jotham's mother being the daughter of the priest might

have instructed and warned him of the consequences of transgressing the laws of God. Of course Jotham had witnessed the predicament of his father, who was struck with leprosy due to disobedience. Jotham might also have been told of what had happened to his grandfathers who started well but ended up in tragedy. Although his father reigned for fifty-two years, half of which were wasted, Jotham's short term reign of sixteen years was much better and well spent in the sight of the Lord. Although he also did not remove the high places, he emphasized the need to acknowledge the Most Holy One.

ELEVENTH GENERATION OF SOLOMON - AHAZ
Deliverance Totally Ignored

2 Kings 16:1-4 reads,

...Ahaz the son of Jotham, king of Judah, began to reign. Ahaz was twenty years old when he became king, and he reigned sixteen years in Jerusalem; and he did not do what was right in the sight of the Lord his God, as his father David had done. But he walked in the way of the kings of Israel;

Indeed he made his son pass through the fire, according to the abominations of the nations whom the Lord had cast out from before the children of Israel. And he sacrificed and burned incense on the high places, on the hills, and under every green tree. Ahaz's reign could be described as the worst of all the kings of Judah. He probably deliberately ignored the laws of God; and desperately provoked God to anger. The sixteen years of his reign were a terror to his own family, especially the children. He was a contrast to the humble God-fearing life of his father Jotham.

TWELFTH GENERATION OF SOLOMON - HEZEKIAH
Deliverance Accepted And Observed

2 Kings 18:1-8,

...**Hezekiah the son of Ahaz, king of Judah began to reign. He was twenty-five years old when he became king, and he reigned twenty-nine years in Jerusalem. His mother's name was Abi the daughter of Zechariah. And he did what was right in the sight of the Lord, according to all that his father David had done. He removed the high places and broke the sacred pillars, cut down the wooden images and broke in pieces the bronze serpent that Moses had made; for until those days the children of Israel burned incense to it, and called it Nehushtan. He trusted in the Lord God of Israel, so that after him was none like him among all the kings of Judah, nor any who were before him. For he held fast to the Lord, he did not depart from following Him, but kept His commandments, which the Lord had commanded Moses. The Lord was with him; he prospered wherever he went. And he rebelled against the king of Assyria and did not serve him. He subdued the Philistines, as far as Gaza and its territory, from watchtower to fortified city.**
[*Underlining by author.*]

It was obvious that Hezekiah was quite displeased with the

manner in which his father had behaved. If God had spared his own life from being offered as a human sacrifice to mundane gods and demons, he had better appreciate it. The great God of wonders had spared and preserved his life for obvious reasons; to keep the promise made to King David. Hezekiah opted for the Most High God. It was a real war against the principalities of darkness in the high places. It was a matter of do or die. He would rather serve the Lord than bow to the demons that destroyed his fathers.

Probably it became a rule to insist that the kings were married to godly women from the priestly families, so that the children could be dedicated to a God-fearing life; and also to be trained to accept and understand the God of their forefathers. Hezekiah's mother was from the priestly home, being the daughter of Zachariah. Hezekiah applied the Word of God thoroughly. He went beyond seeking salvation of his people and that of his own life. He also conducted total deliverance throughout the land of Judah. In fact, he was the only king who was bold enough to destroy the high places built by King Solomon.

The high places harbored the demons and principalities of darkness that constantly attacked the house of David, causing them to backslide. Abi being a virtuous woman of God might have influenced her son to pull down the stronghold of Judah's abomination. Hezekiah's profile is quite challenging. His integrity is close to that of King David. Like his great grand-father David, Hezekiah trusted in the Lord God beyond any reasonable doubt. His trust in God is recorded as being incomparable to this day.

Hezekiah clung very closely to the Lord, and kept the commandments. He studied the laws of God judiciously, and made them applicable to his life. He won the heart of God, and so he enjoyed the presence of God. The Lord also granted him favor of power to subdue his enemies. Like David, Hezekiah was quick to repent; he sought for deliverance on a regular basis to keep up his relationship with the Lord. He never took the laws of the Lord for granted. He respected the ministers of God and their services in the presence of the Lord.

THIRTEENTH AND FOURTEENTH GENERATION OF SOLOMON
Manasseh and Amon Rejected Deliverance

2 Kings 21:1-18,

Manasseh was twelve years old when he became king, and he reigned fifty-five years in Jerusalem. His mother's name was Hephzibah. And he did evil in the sight of the Lord, according to the abominations of the nations whom the Lord had cast out before the children of Israel. For he rebuilt the high places which Hezekiah his father had destroyed; he raised up altars for Baal, and made a wooden image, as Ahab king of Israel had done; and he worshiped all the host of heaven and served them. ...Also he made his son pass through the fire, practiced soothsaying, used witchcraft, and consulted spiritists and mediums. He did much evil in the sight of the Lord, to provoke Him to anger. He even set a carved image of Ashterah that he had made, in the house of which the Lord had said to David and to Solomon his son, "In this house and in Jerusalem, which I have chosen out of all the tribes of Israel, I will put My name forever, ...only if they are careful to do according to all

that I have commanded them, and according to all the law that My servant Moses commanded them. **But they paid no attention, and Manasseh seduced them to do more evil than the nations whom the Lord had destroyed before the children of Israel...**<u>Moreover Manasseh shed much innocent blood, till he had filled Jerusalem from one end to another</u>**, besides his sin with which he made Judah sin, in doing evil in the sight of the Lord... So Manasseh rested with his fathers, and was buried in the garden of his own house, in the garden of Uzza. Then his son Amon reigned in his place.** [*Underlining by author.*]

2 Kings 21:19-26,

Amon was twenty-two years old when he became king, and he reigned two years in Jerusalem. His mother's name was Meshullemeth the daughter of Haruz of Jotbah. <u>And he did evil in the sight of the Lord, as his father Manasseh had done. So he walked in all the ways that his father had walked; and he served the idols that his father had served, and worshiped them.</u> **He forsook the Lord God of his fathers, and did not walk in the way of the Lord. The servants of Amon conspired against him, and killed the king in his own house. ...And he was buried in his tomb in the garden of Uza. Then Josiah his son reigned in his place.** [*Underlining by author.*]

It is sad to note that, while Hezekiah had successfully pulled down the strongholds of Israel's abomination, his son Manasseh who was the immediate successor rebuilt the high places. This encouraged the worship of foreign gods once again. The attitude of Manasseh and Amon (Manasseh's son and successor) portrayed the two of them as the most wicked kings in Judah. They both defiled the temple of the Most Holy God.

Manasseh offered his son for sacrifice to the foreign gods. Manasseh and Amon were a disgrace to their father Hezekiah, who had cherished deliverance and respected the laws of the Lord. In fact Amon was so wicked that his own servants could not tolerate his ungodly behavior; so they conspired and terminated his life.

These two kings, Manasseh and Amon were buried in Uzza's garden. They were not given the honorable obsequies of kingship; neither were they taken near King David's tomb. Their acts were also not recorded in the Chronicles of the Kings of Judah.

Who were their mothers? Were they from the lineage of the foreign women? Were they party to those who harbored and served household gods? Did they ignore the deliverance carried out by the High Priest of the Most High God? These are questions that demand careful examinations and answers, as transgression of the laws of intermarriage to ungodly nations have been the cause of Israel's misbehavior.

FIFTEENTH GENERATION OF SOLOMON - JOSIAH
Deliverance Accepted And Observed

2 Kings 22:1-7 says,

Josiah was eight years old when he

became king, and he reigned thirty-one years in Jerusalem. His mother's name was Jedidah the daughter of Adaiah of Bozkath. And he did what was right in the sight of the Lord, and walked in all the ways of his father David; he did not turn aside to the right hand or to the left. Now it came to pass, in the eighteen year...the king sent Shaphan the scribe...to the house of the Lord, saying, "Go up to Hilkiah the priest, that he may count the money which has been brought into the house of the Lord, which the doorkeepers have gathered from the people. And let them deliver it into the hand of those doing the work, who are the overseers in the house of the Lord...to carpenters and builders and masons - and to buy timber and hewn stone to repair the house. Then Hilkiah the high priest said to Shaphan the scribe, "<u>I have found the Book of the Law in the house of the Lord</u>." ...Now it happened, when the king heard the words of the Book of the Law, that he tore his clothes. Then the king commanded Hilkiah the priest... "<u>Go, inquire of the Lord for me, for the people and for all Judah, concerning the words of this book that has been found; for great is the wrath of the Lord that is aroused against us, because our fathers have not obeyed the words of this book, to do according to all that is written concerning us.</u>" But to the king of Judah who sent you to inquire of the Lord... <u>"because your heart was</u>

tender, and you humbled yourself before the Lord when you heard what I spoke against this place and against its inhabitants, that they would become a desolation and a curse, and you tore your clothes and wept before me, I also have heard you," says the Lord. [*Underlining by author.*]

2 Kings 23 records,

...Then the king stood by a pillar and made a covenant before the Lord to follow the Lord and to keep His commandments and His testimonies and His statutes, with all his heart and all his soul, to perform the words of the covenant that were written in this book. And all the people took their stand for the covenant. And the king commanded Hilkiah the high priest, ...to bring out of the temple of the Lord all the articles that were made for Baal, for Ashterah, and for all the host of heaven; ...the wooden image from the house of the Lord, to the Brook Kidron outside Jerusalem, burned it at the Brook Kidron and ground it to ashes, and threw its ashes to the graves of the common people... Then Josiah also took away all the shrines of the high places that were in the cities of Samaria, which the kings of Israel had made to provoke the Lord to anger; ...He executed all the priests of the high places who were there, on the altars, and burned men's bones on them; and he returned to Jerusalem.

Then the king commanded all the people, saying, "Keep the Passover to the Lord your God, as it is written in this Book of the Covenant. Surely such a Passover had never been held since the days of the judges who judged Israel, nor in all the days of the kings of Israel and the kings of Judah ...Moreover Josiah put away those who consulted mediums and spiritists, the household gods and idols, all the abominations that were seen in the land of Judah and Jerusalem, that he might perform the book that Hilkiah the priest found in the house of the Lord. Now before him there was no king like him, who turned to the Lord with all his heart, with all his soul, and with all his might, according to all the Law of Moses; nor after him did any arise like him. (*Underlining by author.*}

Indeed, it has always been a difficult task for God to find a man who will surrender his total being—spirit, soul and body—to God till the very end. Josiah's revival seems to have outwitted that of any other king in Israel. The fear of God that came upon him shelved the curse and punishment that had been pronounced upon Israel unto another generation. Josiah showed God his zealousness, and intention to lay his life on the altar for the salvation of his people.

He conducted an aggressive deliverance, beyond his own territory, into the land of his brethren in the Northern Kingdom. He destroyed the high places and burnt the remnant into ashes to erase the handwriting of ordinances of powers and principalities of darkness. He also ravaged the homes of individual practitioners to ensure personal idols were not spared. Those who practiced and consulted witches, mediums, sorcerers and spiritists were also dealt with. Josiah encouraged the services of the High Priest, until the laws presented to Moses were executed letter by letter and precept upon precept.

SIXTEENTH, SEVENTEENTH AND EIGHTEENTH GENERATION OF SOLOMON - JEHOAHAZ, JOHOIACHIN AND ZEDEKIAH
Deliverance Rejected And Ignored

Jehoahaz, Johoiachin and Zedekiah were the last three kings of Judah. They did evil in the sight of the Lord. They persecuted and killed the prophets of God (**2 Kings 23:31-37; 24; 25**).

Deliverance and repentance were far from these three kings. They preferred to humiliate the prophets of God rather than obey the warnings meant to avert the punishment coming upon them. Their evil caused them to suffer invasion from foreign kingdoms, and they were carried away into slavery. Their unrepentant lives held them into captivity both in the physical and in the spirit realm. Even when they saw the direction leading toward their freedom, they could not yield because the enemy had blinded them.

One of the major reasons why Jehoiakim was held in bondage was because of the sin of his father Manasseh.

2 Kings 24:2-4 states,

...Surely at the commandment of the Lord this came upon Judah, to remove them from His sight because of the innocent blood that he had shed; for he had filled Jerusalem with innocent blood, which the Lord would not pardon."

Poetic Expression Four

WAR AGAINST SPIRITUAL CAPTIVITY

War against spiritual captivity
I shall not entertain astrology
I shall believe in the Almighty God
I shall learn His precepts
I shall abide in His Word
I shall not go astray
I shall not surrender to deception
I shall war against spiritual captivity.

War against spiritual captivity
I shall not entertain fortunetellers
Away with the mediums
Away with the crystalists
Away with the palmists
Away with rituals
I shall hold on to Jesus Christ
I shall war against spiritual captivity.

War against spiritual captivity
I shall not entertain witchcraft
Away with witch-hunting
I shall find fault with no one
Away with confusion
I shall accuse no one
Away with interference
I shall war against spiritual captivity

War against spiritual captivity
I shall not entertain evil spirits
I shall subdue the enemy
I shall make a public show of him

I shall renounce satanic ordinances
I shall fear no foe
I shall possess my authority
I shall overcome spiritual captivity.

War against spiritual captivity
No more shall I be held in captivity
No more shall I be held in captivity
No more shall I be held in bondage
My soul is free from prison
I am released to praise my Maker
My soul is free from death
I am released to worship Him
Indeed I have conquered spiritual captivity.

Pauline Walley, November 1996

Chapter Four

SPIRITUAL CAPTIVITY

Isaiah 61:1:

...To preach good tidings to the poor...

One major ministry of our Lord and Savior Jesus Christ as indicated in the Book of Isaiah is to deliver those in captivity and bondage. As far back as the days of the Old Testament, it was prophesied that Jesus Christ was coming to deliver. **Isaiah 61:1 says, "The Spirit of the Lord is upon Me; because He has anointed Me to preach good tidings to the poor; He has sent me to heal the broken-hearted, to proclaim liberty to the captive, and the opening of prison to those who are bound."**

Also in the New Testament, **Luke 4:18-19 is repeated,**

> **The Spirit of the Lord God is upon Me, because He has anointed Me to preach the gospel to the poor. He has sent Me to heal the broken-hearted, to preach deliverance to the captives And recovery of sight to the blind, to set at liberty those who are**

**oppressed, to preach the acceptable year
of the Lord.**

These passages give a clear indication that deliverance
ministration was part of the teaching and demonstration of
our Lord Jesus Christ, who also came unto us as an example.
In order to give detailed meaning and understanding to the
above passages, some of the reasons stated are discussed. In
this chapter, the various forms of deliverance are discussed
in details. Some real life examples and testimonies are cited
with or without the real names of the persons involved. In
cases where permission has not been sought or granted, an
unusual name will be replaced for the sake of confidentiality.

It is pertinent to use some of these instances to prove the
reality of the nature of the issues that are discussed in this
book; especially because many people do not quite understand what goes on in the realms of the spirit.

PROCLAMATION OF LIBERTY TO THE CAPTIVES

Isaiah 61:1,

**...To proclaim liberty to the captives, and
the opening of prison to them that are
bound...**

The question is: Who are the captives? Where are they?
Where could they be found? What do they look like? How
do we know that they are captives and are in bondage? Now,
let it be known that the captives are everywhere, wherever
man is. There are captives in every denominational gathering ("the Church") and outside the assembly. Since Jesus
came for the unrighteous, to the lost sheep, then there is no
particular boundary.

However, there are issues that makes one a captive. Thus, one could be held captive by various reasons, through various means. One can either be held in spiritual captivity, physical captivity, material captivity, emotional captivity, secular captivity and/or financial captivity. This is because, the enemy, in a desperate bid to catch the attention of Christians, walk to and fro the earth, seeking various means to hold people in bondage. Although the Scripture mentions various forms of captivity, little is known to the brethren. Many are fond of holding on to the portions of Scriptures that suit them, or convenient for their actions or lifestyle.

The truth about who a captive is and how one gets into captivity will amaze you as you read this book. When you discover the truth about yourself, don't rebel; don't react; stay cool; examine your past and present; confess and repent. By so doing, you will be making headway to establish your foundation in the kingdom of God.

WHAT IS CAPTIVITY?

Captivity is a state of being held by force under an unwilling situation to which one did not actually give consent; such as in slavery, imprisonment, servitude, bondage, confinement, dungeon or jail. Sometimes, people could be held captive as a result of offense committed directly or indirectly. Some also do give themselves up for captivity because they think there are no better choices in life than to accept anything. There are cases when people deliberately walk into captivity, despising laid-down rules or appropriate precautions that could prevent the possibility of becoming a captive. Also, there are cases where innocent persons are captured and put under forced labor, which is often the case of slavery.

WHO IS A CAPTIVE?

Mankind stepped into captivity the day he was deceived in the Garden of Eden. By eating from the forbidden tree, mankind voluntary exchanged the life of God in him, for the spiritual death in Satan. As a result, mankind was driven out of the Garden, which represented the kingdom of God, and began to wander about on earth.

Having been driven out, mankind lost fellowship with God. The regular enjoyment of the presence of God was lost. Mankind became a prey in the mouth of Satan, the devourer. Mankind became entangled with the works of the flesh, as the consciousness of the presence of God was no longer there. The less consciousness of the Holy Spirit gave opportunity for Satan to increase his deceptive devices on mankind.

Satan got hold of mankind, and held him in bondage as a captive in his camp. He influenced mankind to live in sin and adapt his lifestyle to the works of the flesh. Even when mankind is convicted of sin, he thinks it is his right to defend his action. For instance, Cain ignored the warning of the Holy Spirit when he purposed in his heart to kill his brother Abel. Cain was rude to God when he was convicted about the sin of murder committed against Abel. When asked the whereabouts of his brother Abel, feeling justified and complacent, he said, "Am I my brother's keeper?" Satan capitalized on Cain's weakness, until he became a vagabond on earth.

The state of Cain could be described as one who consciously walked into captivity. He openly gave his life to Satan, despite the warning of the Holy Spirit. He openly surrendered himself to Satan to be held captive, when he avoided the warning and went ahead to kill his brother. Just like his parent, Cain did not repent, although God gave him the opportunity to do so. Despite the fact that he knew the voice of God, and did recognize the presence of God, and did respond to whatever God said to him, yet, he did not repent. He preferred to be a slave to sin. So Satan held him in bondage as a captive.

Like Cain, many people do claim to hear the voice of God. Some of these people are religious and active workers within church buildings. Some of these Cain-like types of individuals are motivators and leaders in our churches, yet they are slaves to sin. Hence, their lives are under the bondage of Satan, having been held captive by the works of the flesh. Therefore, a captive is anyone who has no easy control over the works of the flesh. A captive is a person who is easily manipulated by the works of the flesh; one who is neither hot nor cold, here nor there; one whose desires are controlled by circumstances; and one who is more sensitive to the things that pertain to worldly cares. A self-contained person is a slave to sin. This explains the simple meaning of a life being held in bondage.

SPIRITUAL CAPTIVITY

Spiritual captivity has to do with indulgence in occultism, and spiritualization with powers and principalities of darkness in high places. These include involvement with mediums, sorcery, palmistry, astrology, crystal ball reading, witchcraft/witchdoctor, Voodoo, Rastafarianism, Africanism, Eastern religions, the New Age Movement, etc.

There are different types of spiritual captivity. One can be held in captivity through indulgence either by practice, or consultation; it can also be through territorial control whereby the dwellers or nationals of a certain community or neighborhood are controlled by a particular set of demons and powers of principalities of darkness in high places. In such cases, the people are influenced by a common trait of behaviors and characters as will be seen in the next chapter on *Physical Captivity*. A community may exhibit a belief system that is strange and sometimes considered as religious or traditional. Sometimes spiritual captivity could lead a whole nation into a system of worship considered to be cultural or ancestral; meanwhile, it has a demonic connotation.

Also, the vicinity or neighborhood in which a particular occult is practiced is often ruled and controlled by the powers and principalities in charge of that occult. People who live within that vicinity do suffer demonic interferences that do hinder their progress in life. People are either haunted until they compromise, or move out of such communities. A person's soul could be captured if one walks into such a territory carelessly. Once a person steps into a demonic controlled territory, one suffers some form of attack that gives an unusual feeling, frustration, depression or sickness. A prayerful Christian will sense the difference in the feel of the atmosphere.

Once this is noticed, there is a need to seek deliverance to wage off the attack. For the war is not against flesh and blood but against powers and principalities of darkness in high places. If an immediate action is not taken, the enemy will strengthen its forces and subdue the person until he/she begins to yield to sin or compromise with some beliefs that are "religiously" demonic. This could lead to backsliding in silence (neither cold nor hot) or walking out of church. A soul in satanic captivity begins to suffer demonic control, because a little delay leads to massive attack and destruction at the least opportunity. An active Christian suddenly begins to misbehave, and express doubts about the Word of God. Sometimes such a person holds on to doctrines that are less profitable to salvation.

MEDIUM

A medium is a person who communicates with the dead or with evil spirits. Such persons claim to have access to the dead by means of certain practices, which are unholy in the sight of God. Mediums dictate the life of the consulters through predictions. They are the type of satanic agents that captures people's souls and begin to monitor them at will for their own benefit. The Bible warns that people who act as mediums and their consulters should not be allowed to exist.

Leviticus 20:6-8,

And the person who turns after mediums and familiar spirits, to prostitute himself with them, I will set My face against that person and cut him off from his people. Sanctify yourselves therefore, and be holy, for I am the Lord your God. And you shall keep my status and perform them; I am the Lord who sanctifies you.

SORCERER

A sorcerer is someone who performs magical works for evil purposes. **Exodus 22:18 says, "You shall not permit a sorcerer to live."**

PALMIST

A palmist is one who reads the palm to tell people about matters that affect their lives.

ASTROLOGER

An astrologer is one who tells the future through stargazing. It is one of the many demonic channels through which people's souls are arrested and held in captivity. It is a regular practice for people, including "Christians" to buy newspapers in the morning with the intention of reading their stars. Many people believe strongly in starting their day off with reading their star. These persons will not dabble into anything until they have checked what the stars say. They live and abide by the word of the astrologer. Their lives and decisions are based on the information gathered from astrological predictions. They see astrology predictions as a type of prophetic word; but it is a false prophecy.

Anyone involved in star reading is being controlled by the demons in charge of the month to which one is attached. There are principalities of darkness in charge of certain times and seasons of the months as allocated by the spirit of deception. The principalities of darkness, like the prince of Persia controls people born at a particular times of the year. Satan is aware that the human mind is curious. Since mankind was originally created in the image of God, humans have the tendency of wanting to know the mind of God concerning their daily endeavors. Hence Satan uses zodiac stars to influence the human mind, such as: Aries (March 21-April 19), Taurus (April 20-May 20), Capricorn (December 22-January 19), Leo (July 23-August 22), etc. Readers and believers of astrology are controlled, guided and protected by demons, powers and principalities of darkness in high places.

In fact, since the astrologers deal with principalities in the sky, demons are just ordinary messengers of the principalities. Therefore, the star readers are in the captive chains of the principalities that control them. When you pick up the newspaper or the book that carries these messages, you will notice how ugly and satanic the faces of the pictures are. Anyone who reads the Zodiac writings is in Zodiac captivity. No matter how active you are in the house of the Lord, you are just a religious person. You don't have the control of the Holy Spirit but that of Satan through the Zodiac powers. You believe it, so you rely on it to tell you what your day or month will look like. You are not a Christian, you are just trying to be one if you are strongly attached to star reading. You need to repent, and confess your sins. It is totally satanic.

CRYSTALIST

The Crystalist is one who uses the crystal ball to perform oracles, such as reading the future through the crystal ball, bathe people with the crystal ball and do all sorts of things with the crystal. This is ungodly, and it is a form of competition with the Holy Spirit. Any time you live within the boundary of the church, and cross over to the crystalist territory, you offer your soul to the principalities in charge of the crystal, and so you are held captive, until the day you repent, and confess.

WITCHCRAFT/WITCH DOCTOR

A witch is one who practices black magic. Such a person is seen as wicked and dangerous, as she is involved in destruction of lives and invention of catastrophe. Their motives are dirty and frightening. The witch doctor is one who professes to heal people by using diabolical means, which are devilish. The witch doctor is often seen as a confusionist, who often destroys the consulter's family, rather than provide solution to problems. The Scripture says witches shall not inherit the kingdom of heaven. Jezebel is described as a witch in **2 Kings 9:22** because she contended with the prophets of God and killed them. Manasseh is described as an evil king, because he consulted soothsayers and witchcraft.

2 Chronicles 33:6,

...He caused his sons to pass through the fire in the Valley of the son of Hinnom; he practiced soothsaying, used witchcraft and sorcery, and consulted mediums and spiritists. He did much evil in the sight of the Lord, to provoke Him to anger.

TESTIMONY

Sharon is about 7 years old this year. Sharon was sent to her paternal grandmother while she was just about 3 years of age. Unfortunately for her mum, Sharon's Aunty, Lana was involved in witchcraft. As part of her wicked devices, Aunty Lana imparted the spirit of witchcraft into the young girl - Sharon.

Innocent Sharon was then mandated to inflict her parents with poverty and family separation. Sharon was also given power to fly at night. Her powers enabled her to fly from one city of the world to another just to carry out a devilish mission. With this, she was able to fly from the city of Accra to London. Although she is young in the physical, yet she is "great" in spiritual wickedness. To a certain extent, Sharon succeeded in accomplishing the satanic mission assigned to her.

Fortunately, the problems her mother Sylvia encountered as a result of the witchcraft spell, led her to surrender her life to Jesus. Sylvia's husband, who is also Sharon's dad, suddenly disappeared from home and began to live on his own without any form of misunderstanding. Secondly, Sylvia's finances began to dwindle without much expenditure.

Suddenly, Sylvia felt it was time to bring Sharon around and tutor her in the things of God, since she is now a dedicated Christian. On arrival, Sylvia noted the strange behavior of Sharon, among others in the family. This strange behavior led to the discovery of the witchcraft spell that Sharon has inherited from Aunty Lana. All attempts to get Sharon to renounce her indulgence met stiff opposition until 2 years after, when Sharon was brought to my house for ministration.

The Spirit of conviction of sin came upon Sharon as we shared with her the love of Jesus. Sharon renounced her involvement and gave her life to Jesus Christ that night of July 7th, 1996, before I left for the Caribbean. After her conversion, the little girl Sharon wrote a letter to Jesus Christ asking for divine protection. Below is an unedited version of Sharon's letter that night.

"Dear God cover me Sharon with the blood of Jesus and let your angels protect me in Jesus name I pray Amen."

For the first time in about two years, Sharon smiled and laughed after her deliverance. Her countenance changed and she became cheerful that night. In the words of her mom Sylvia, "I never knew that my daughter was this intelligent. I had no idea that she could write so well and talk like this. Apparently, the witchcraft spirit prevented her from paying attention to her academics in class. Now I know what it means to be bedeviled by witchcraft."

ANALYSIS

It is very important to note that no evil spirit is merciful toward anyone. Once you enter the trap of a witch, you are in danger of one sort of bondage or another. Can you imagine that a young girl of about the age of three could be used to destroy her own parents? Would anyone ever believe that such an evil behavior does exist? Yes, that is the result of spiritual captivity. We need to be watchful and sensitive to the things of the spirit rather than to the things of the flesh.

OBEAH: THE CARIBBEAN TERMINOLOGY FOR WITCHCRAFT

Obeah is the common terminology for witchcraft in the Caribbean. The practice is common and handled with a lot of diplomacy. Both the consulters and the practitioners are held in high esteem and in secrecy, probably because of fear of falling victim to their spell. People hardly talk about the obeah man or woman in public. A mention of the word itself is terrific, as it sends shivers into the spines of people around. Below is a piece on the operation of witchcraft culled from a magazine.

OBEAH IN JAMAICA

Of lotions, potions, oils of love and oils of stay by Paulette McDonald (*Lifestyle, Nov/Dec. 1990 pp.7-13*). When I was a little girl, there was a man in the rural district who stole fowls. He would pluck them and display them for sale on a wire hoop at the market. I saw him once and still remember my bizarre fascination with the helpless looking and naked birds hanging by their necks. I also still remember what happened to him.

One day there was a confrontation at the "cross roads" between the thief and a woman who raised fowls. She was waving a stick at him and accompanied by a torrent of expletives she told him if he did not stop taking her stock she was going to "fix him up" with a fowl's beak.

Not long after the public threat, the man developed a pimple at the corner of his mouth, which grew progressively worse despite all efforts to heal it. It ate away at his flesh and healed only when both lips took on a pointed shape. It was my first exercise in real terror and confusion. In retrospect I think it was probably easier on the man that he also lost his mind. Thereafter he had no more interest in stealing anything at all.

As often as this kind of experience is duplicated all over Jamaica and the Caribbean, there is also the corresponding story of people who were given "nine days" to live and who either died on the 10th or escaped the spell at the hands of some obeah man. To say that obeah is prevalent in Jamaica is like repeating the religious denomination to which the Pope belongs.

Some believe in it and others do not. Some will deal in it with one hand and deny its efficacy with the other. What is clear however is that for everybody, obeah is an embarrassment; something one does not admit to utilizing, and something in which only the lower class and the unintelligent indulge in, or so we would think! Very few will ever admit they ever sought the services of a "daddy," a "father," a "medda," or a "bishop" as obeah-men (used to mean also obeah-women) are called; that they ever went deep into a rural area (or a yard in Kingston) in the dead of night or at the crack of dawn searching for the telltale red flag on the bamboo pole which marks the obeah-man's workshop.

What is also clear is that the obeah-man is still giving succor and support to thousands of Jamaicans. Day after day, many people who could be described as middle class, educated, and intelligent do seek out the obeah-man, who may himself be an illiterate; to trust him with their most private business, and to trust in the advice he gives. People use obeah for many reasons: to get promotion at work, to triumph in a court case, to secure the love of a straying spouse or lover, to become prosperous, to stop others from becoming prosperous, to recover their health, to set evil spirits on their enemies, to remove evil spirits from themselves and to KILL, among a range of other things.

The business of killing however, splits obeah-men into two distinct ranks—those who believe in God and use Him as a medium to heal and bring success and prosperity to their clients, and those who use the devil as a medium for their work. It is evident what they do. The former kind is put in a group which some people call "myal men."

The healers and surveyors of success and prosperity also use the oils and perfumes a "myal man" may use, but for different objectives. The healers make a point of giving the "client" a reading—looking mysteriously through a glass of water, a crystal ball, "splitting" tarot cards or looking at certain parts of the Bible, especially the Psalms. They claim to be able to see in the future and can tell about the present and the past. Following their diagnosis, they make a prescription, which they either buy themselves or send the "patient" to a drug store (usually not called a pharmacy) to buy.

The "myal men" also claim to be able to see into the future, etc., but do not necessarily have to read. Clients can only be going to them for one thing. But even though there is a split in their ranks, they are all loosely called obeah-men and it is necessary for their paths to converge at a point because the healer and lifter of evil spells must know something about the casting of the spells in order to be able to remove them.

Sometimes it is necessary to put his entire "career" on the line and risk his life to fight the greater evil, but he will not employ evil means. He must work in the confidence that good must triumph over evil. It is not unusual for these "good" obeah-men to fail and for the patient to die. In cases where this happens, this man's reputation and skill comes under serious question and he may lose the support of some or all of his other patients.

Obeah-men are like doctors and are in many cases better paid. It is also not unusual for a man to take his obeah-man to court rather than his lawyer. In many ways too, the balm yard is like a hospital with patients waiting hours for attention. People sit quietly at the obeah-man's. They do not trade stories about "pressure," "sugar" and the like. Mysterious personal problems are embarrassing, so each person sits in silence with the heavy burden of his problems etched on his face. There are rarely any happy faces at the balm yard. It appears as if obeah-men base their success on a strange and curious confluence of coincidence, faith and a little bit of luck. Many people who have claimed to be healed appear to have already set the stage for their healing in their minds. Some go to the medical doctor first and then in their impatience go to the obeah-man and give the credit for the improvement to the obeah-men. The only real ability that an obeah-man may seem to possess is his knowledge of herb remedies for which he can earn a great reputation. But many Jamaicans from all strata of society who visit these men and swear by their work would probably disagree.

Obeah is defined as a superstitious belief that certain men and women can exercise supernatural powers over places, persons and things and can produce effects beyond men's control. The word is derived from Hebrew— *Obimena*, a snake, with which people in the earlier days used to work. The practice itself is said to have arisen in Egypt and then spread over the African continent.

Abraham Ettrick, a Catholic priest who served in Jamaica after the abolition of slavery, wrote in his book, Obeah and Duppyism in Jamaica; that the slaves brought obeah to Jamaica hidden in their hair. So hair was routinely shaved by frightened slave traders. Very few people are not frightened by the thought that they could be hurt by obeah. They still shiver at stories about strange happenings or about people who were supposedly killed by obeah-men.

Obeah is a little bit of everything. Its subtext is about duppies, graves, superstitions, evil spells, death, oils, powders and perfumes. The basic ideology, however, is rooted in religion and devil worship. People who use obeah see it as a means of protecting themselves against evil and in a weird kind of way, "obtaining justice" for real or imagined infractions against them.

Jamaicans are a very religious people and it is mainly because of this highly religious profile in the society that people believe in this kind of supernatural action—a kind of miracle. Jamaicans are also a very hopeful people, no matter how hard the times are. This hope and faith is heard in the timeless songs they sing at funerals and at church about "meeting loved ones on the other side" and of preparations being made by God to make them comfortable in the after life.

Though Jamaicans believe ardently in God, there is also a feeling of self-satisfaction to believe that in the meantime and until He returns, there are "ordained" men and women, ordinary mortals who supposedly can act on their behalf "giving justice" to those who have somehow wronged them. Those people who deliberately go to put evil spells on others have a twisted way of thinking that this is also justice and that God will somehow forgive is weighted in statements such as: "God helps those who help themselves." or "God says you must go out and seek a physician."

A popular saying in tenement brawls is *"lawd missis me no wan' you go carry me name go a cotton tree."* This is of special significance.

The cotton tree is one of the media through which the obeah-men work, especially the "myal men." They are believed to be able to kill or injure anyone, for a fee—visiting cemeteries at nights and calling up spirits to do their work. The "myal men" harm by "depriving people of their shadow" or setting duppies on them. When the shadow is taken, it is carried and nailed to, or buried under the cotton tree. The person involved is never healthy and pines away until death unless the shadow is returned in a complex ritual by another obeah-man.

Many may remember when the big cotton tree at the foot of Authur Wint Drive was taken away or fell down because of old age. A great deal of excitement was generated when hundreds of pieces of paper were found with the names of judges, lawyers and other prominent people in society. Consultant psychiatrist at the Bellevue Hospital, Dr. Aggrey Irons, believes obeah-men are charlatans. He says people believe in obeah because of the traditional habit of looking to external sources for the causes and solutions to their problems.

Dr. Irons says he has seen many patients who come in for treatment and, if pressed, will say they believe that they are ill because someone "worked obeah" on them. So why do they come to the hospital then? "That is usually after they have been to the obeah-man and they still hear the voices in their heads," he said.

He agrees that there may be a connection between the physical and the metaphysical, but he says obeah-men try to exploit this without even understanding the full extent of the connection. In fact, he says, obeah-men and some kinds of churches in Jamaica thrive on the belief systems of people, extracting exorbitant sums of money in the process.

The buying and selling of obeah is now as prevalent in the corporate area as it is in the rural areas. A friend who has a stall in one of Kingston's arcades said that she would not have done as well in sales if she had not "gone out" to get "fix up". She says it is a regular practice for people to sprinkle powders and oils at the stalls of other vendors and for fights to break out and "word throwing" to take place. She has joined the daily ritual of the cheese pan with blue water (a blue tablet used to whiten clothes) mixed with lime, which is routinely splashed around the stall area every morning before any business is conducted. This is said to reduce the effect of any obeah, which is set overnight.

Another area of Jamaican life in which obeah is used for protection and success is in the entertainment business. DJs commonly accuse each other of working obeah on each other to prevent records from selling. Admiral Bailey has a popular song *"Science Again"* and it is said the song was not done as commentary alone. The mother and girlfriend of another popular DJ are said to visit the obeah-man frequently to keep their love relationship on the charts. Obeah is so powerful in the Jamaican culture that an unsuccessful candidate in last year's general elections pointed out that people could change their preference under the threat of obeah.

My neighbor's helper told me two of her experiences. She was working at one time with a woman who ran a shop and a bar. One day she was cleaning the freezer when she found a frozen sausage can with tiny pieces of rolled up paper in it. She could not make out what was written on the paper as the ink was blurred, but she became suspicious and related her finding to her colleague next door. *"You neva know say yoyu missis a big obeah worker…must be people pikney name she have inna har freezer a cold-up,"* the next-door maid confided upon hearing that she threw the can away. She was fired a few days after her employer missed the item.

When she was a young girl she was given nine days to live by a woman over a romantic altercation. She began to feel weak, listless and disoriented. She went to the obeah-man first; and he told her she would die, and charged her $1,000 to lift the spell. A few months after she visited a doctor for a "female problem," the doctor told her she had "iron poor blood" and prescribed iron tablets. To this day she never made the connection between the anemia and the weak and listless feeling. She gave all the credit to the obeah-man.

PAULETTE McDONALD'S PERSONAL EXPERIENCE

My first experience with an obeah-man occurred one Sunday in late May as I sought material for this article. I headed for St.

Thomas with a higgler from whom I bought foodstuff regularly. She knew vaguely why I wanted to go, but told me I may very well benefit from the experience as I had never "gone out." She prepared me thus: No pants, my head should be covered with a hat or scarf and I would not be admitted if I went alone. We boarded a mini-bus at 5:45 a.m., and I felt everyone on the bus knew where I was going. We walked up a long hill before we came to a church with a wooden building in the back. Long, wooden benches such as those seen in a rural clinic or church were available for the clients or patients to sit on. Six people were ahead of us. I walked up to a long pole and at its base were whitewashed stones, cacti and freshly cut croton branches in empty white rum bottles.

A fat woman with an elaborate scarlet head wrap and two yellow pencils sticking from behind her ears instructed me to circle the formation which she called a "standard" three times. I was dizzy when I sat down and thought I must have gone around it more than thrice.

We were joined by more people and when I was leaving, near midway, I noticed about six expensive cars parked on the hill. The man peered intently at me and then into a glass of water. He made Chinese-looking characters in an exercise book and told me solemnly what was happening in my life. He was a bent old man, anywhere between 60 and 80 years old. His hair was white, his skin black and leathery, his eyes red and he wore faded khaki pants and a white shirt. The most memorable thing about him was that he was obviously short of breath and had a terrible wheeze. I sympathized with him when he told me that his condition was a result of absorbing some of the evil he had removed from people.

He looked in the glass and told me I had a good job and would soon get a promotion. He said spirits were "playing" with me, then invoked a sexual connotation to the word "playing." He told me I was going to be involved in a scandal, that I would be rich and that I had one child (I do). The most serious diagnosis was about the spirit and he gave me a page from an exercise book to write down a prescription, part of which was also for the promotion:

- 4 inches virgin parchment
- Compellance perfume
- Runaway perfume
- Commanding perfume
- Oil of love/oil of stay
- Sit down perfume
- High John the conqueror
- Runaway oil
- Subduing powder/perfume
- Releasing powder
- Oil of sweet rose
- Musk oil.

In addition, I was to bring a young pigeon for a blood bath, a dressmaker's measuring tape which I would wear around my waist at nights; and he advised me I would need a drinking gourd and a solid gold or silver ring as a guard against evil. When I got up to leave, he rose too. He held my shoulder, spun me around (I guess three times again) and made the mark of the cross on my chest and back with his fore finger and told me not to look back. Of course I never filled the prescription and never went back, but I found that I did not dislike him. He was not offensive. He was benign and he meant no one any harm.

However, my next experience frightened and disturbed me. I did not speak so much of this one as I had never before felt that I was in the presence of such an evil force in my life! This was in Kingston and this man had a multi-colored head wrap and an elaborate robe. I could see the legs of his trousers under the robe. He was small, his eyes were like a snake and his hands were small and looked unlike the man in St. Thomas, like he did no hard work. His actions were effeminate and I suspected that he had never had a close relationship with a woman. Several young boys were hanging around his yard, asking people what they wanted.

He had an irritating stare as if he could see into my very soul and a way of constantly sucking air through his teeth. He spoke perfect English. I spent half-an-hour telling him that I wanted to get rid of a girl who was competing for my boyfriend's attention. He looked at me so long and hard I thought he was about to chase me out. My palms were sweating and I fought hard to keep my hands from shaking.

"What do you want me to do?" he asked in a low deadly voice. Well, I told him, I hated the girl and wanted her "removed."

"What do you want me to do? ...You have to make up your mind," he said.

"Kill her!" I quickly blurted out. He must have looked at me for a full five minutes.

"You said it was someone you knew?" I nodded.

"Can you get a piece of her underwear? ...It can be a slip or a brassiere too."

"But what would that do," I stammered.

I looked at him then, and something like impatience or anger flashed across his face. "You want me to do the work for you or not?" he asked. I nodded again.

"You will give me $50 now," he said, "and the job will cost $2,000."

I left telling him I would be back. His image disturbed me for the rest of the week.

I spoke to the operator of a Kingston drugstore who does a thriving business "fulfilling prescriptions" for obeah cures. He told me most of the products he sells come from a company in Chicago and some are bought locally. He told me that sales from these products outstripped sales of regular prescription drugs. Coming closest to that were sales from Irish moss, linseed and "icing glass" used to make a brew which small traders buy, boil, and bottle as an aphrodisiac which some men swear by.

He insisted that his products were authentic, although he could not measure the success as people never really reported back to him. Sometimes he says he sells in bulk to several men and women who he suspects deal in obeah and he attends to them personally. He points out that his products are not sold with the intention of harming anyone.

However a former employee from another drugstore on Spanish Town Road told me the products were not authentic and that the people who buy them are being taken for a ride. He remembers many occasions when he would pour the same liquid in two different bottles, calling it two different names. He had a scare one day when one woman opened both bottles, smelled them and declared loudly that she was given the wrong "prescription." He tried to convince her, but she insisted and told him she knew that a certain one should be green. He pretended that a genuine mistake had been made, took one of them back and mixed with it the first green liquid he saw on the shelf in the back room. She went away, smiling and satisfied.

Many of us will still ask the question, "Does obeah really work?" The people who trudge through the hills and valleys of Jamaica taking the risk of being see…those who ride their bicycles, those who drive their big expensive cars to the obeah-man, those who have been "healed," have had success, the job promotion, who have secured the affection of a loved one by giving him strange potions, those who know people who have been killed at the hands of a

Jamaican obeah-man would give a collective and resounding answer—"YES!!!"

For them, the words of a song by Loving-deer that some people may consider absolutely hilarious, are true:

> **Oil a tan ya**
> **Oil a leave ya**
> **Oil a mek yu get U.S visa**
> **Oil a me natty hair get curly**
> **Oil a mek man strap girly, girly**
> **Oil a kil rat, roach and fly**
> **Oil a mek politician stop lie.**

WATER SPIRIT

This has to do with the use of holy water, salt water, colored water (green, yellow, blue, red seawater) and such for healing, protection, bathing, and drinking as a means of reaching out to whatever religious spirit is being conjured. It is devilish.

This also involves the use of various colors of candles for prayers, as well as the use of incense. It is nothing but the practice of divination.

RASTAFARIANISM

Rastafarianism is not the national religion or traditional belief of Jamaica. It is an adopted cult practiced by a few who could be far less than 2,000 persons. And so is the dreadlock hairstyle named after Bob Marley (the late reggae star artist). The dreadlock is part of the identification of cult members, although non-cult members who claim to be admirers also wear the hairstyle. However, it has been noted that people who wear the dreadlocks do manifest some sort of serpentine spirits during deliverance ministration.

In recent times, the dreadlock has been modified into more fashionable hairstyles that are neat, attractive and with great artistic designs. The neat and fashionable ones do not carry demons. The dirty dreadlocks that are religiously kept for cult reasons can be irritating and sometimes dangerous because of connection to evil spirits. Beryl M. Allen (*Jamaica, A Junior History*, 1993, p. 55) writes, "Rastafarianism is both a religion and a way of life. Unlike other beliefs, Rastafarianism began in Jamaica. This movement began mainly in the poor sections of towns where life was hard and the majority of people were unemployed."

Rastafarians believe that Ras Tafari is God and that black people can find salvation by going back to Africa. Much of Jamaica's development in music (especially reggae) and art came from members of the Rastafarian belief. Some Rastafarians wear their hair in locks and wear a beard. Different groups of Rastafarians have different beliefs, but all believe that Ras Tafari is God. Rastafarians call their God "Jah." Other cult groups that wear hairstyles that have demonic implications are practitioners of **Voodooism, Hinduism, Afrikanism, Martial Arts, etc.**

The deceptive means by which people are led into captivity is through the reading of books like the sixth or seventh books of Moses, metaphysics, transcendental meditation, astral travel, martial arts, hypnotism, tarot cards, ouija board and some others. Read about the man who was once involved in all sorts of meditation including metaphysics below.

ENTANGLEMENT

A person could be held in spiritual captivity through direct or indirect involvement with practitioners and masters to various occultic groups around the world. Direct involvement is when one deliberately and knowingly expresses desires for such, and belief in mystical activities. Some individuals make it a normal habit to visit secret cults, to make consultation and submit themselves to mystical demands. Deliberate or undeliberate interactions with the practitioners could lead to corruption or contamination.

Indirect involvement is when a person is lured into it ignorantly, or through deception by agents of a particular cultic group. Sometimes one's soul is sold to the devil through ancestral or parental involvement in some form of occultism. It could also be by mere curiosity or consultation. There are various forms of contamination in various parts of the world. It could be through ancestral inheritance or by birth, through relationships or friendship, through culture and traditions (marriage, libation) as well as parental contamination.

The involvement of a parent in an occult does affect other members of the family. Most children love to do what they watch and see their parents do. It is natural for children to learn from their parents. Of course, the home is the first institution of learning, while the parent is the first teacher. In this regard, some curious children attempt to experiment with the things they see their parents do in secret.

Either directly or indirectly, children are indoctrinated or induced to follow the footsteps of their parents in the realm of occultism. These innocent children are then held in bondage to strange cultic practices. They sometimes grow up doing worse things than what their parents ever did.

In cases where the parents are involved, there is an attempt to give some form of false protection to the children. Here, some children are taught to chant or recite some sort of incantation; some are given portions of concoctions to drink; some are given a bath; some are also taught to read, fly at night, and travel out of their body. Many children born to parents involved in occultism often indulge in worse forms of mysticism.

Also, there are cases where names of children are written and dedicated to demons and spirits. Here, it takes the grace of God for such children to be delivered, as their souls have been sold into occultic bondage. In families where the children are not willing participants, such children may not openly renounce indulgence to embarrass their parent, but cling to the Lord Jesus Christ and pray for the salvation of their parents. Although they were indirect participants, these category of persons need deliverance ministration to set their soul free from parental sacrifices to occultic spirits and demons.

It is very important to note that some of these innocent children who refuse to cooperate with their parents' occultic indulgence do suffer serious harassment from the enemy who tries to draw their attention. Some are inflicted with sicknesses, diseases, and all sorts of incurable ailments; some also suffer mental torture, which lands them into the psychiatric hospital. Unfortunately, most psychiatric cases are results of demonic influences and occultic partnership.

TESTIMONY

During the period when I was holding evangelistic crusades and revival meetings in the Caribbean, I came across individuals who were victims of parental indulgence. Particularly was Macia (name changed for confidentiality) who narrated her case in agony. This testimony was published in PWCC's quarterly *Newsletter* of **September to December 1996.**

Macia: I was brought up in a very strict religious family, with five brothers and four sisters. We attended the Anglican Church with our parents. My childhood was pretty normal but sometimes disturbing. My parents, though well meaning, unknowingly dabbled into occultic matters. They read horoscopes; mixed up potions; read the Psalms and turned the Bible face downwards; entered the house backwards after 6:00 p.m, and sprinkled certain substances to keep away evil spirits. This was the background into which we were brought up.

My parents told us of demonic encounters and astral travel but referred to them as "spirits". This drove fear into our hearts and affected me terribly. I had horrible nightmares and would wake up in the night screaming about the snakes on my bed. My mother would comfort me and insert a foul-smelling brown substance in my hair, and I would go back to sleep. The atmosphere around our home was charged with demonic activities as a distant relative practiced witchcraft. Some of our nights were interrupted by weird noises and activities.

As I grew up the fear increased and I started to experience seizure-like pains on the right side of my head. They were so intense that I sometimes blacked out. In order to stay conscious, I would hold tightly to whatever was near to me so as not to fall. I was always under stress, became easily tired, restless, nervous, and sometimes depressed. My life was affected in every aspect.

By this time, I had given my life to the Lord, but was not delivered yet. My life seemed all right on the surface, but deep inside I was uncertain of really who I was. Confused, I consulted several knowledgeable medical people who put me through grueling tests and prescribed medication, which only masked the real symptoms; but the real cause was still there.

Only a Christian psychologist offered hope through the Word. He started the deliverance process by going into my background. I did get deliverance in some areas of my life. For instance I was sexually molested as a child by a relative. Praise God when a friend invited me to come and hear Sister Pauline Walley preach at New Life Tabernacle in Kendal Hill, I accepted eagerly.

From the very first night, my eyes were opened spiritually. It was the same Word but was explained with such authority and power. I could sense God's Holy Spirit and anointing, and as I went forward some of these chains that had bound me started to snap; although initially I did not want to step forward. God was delivering me from these bondages.

The enemy tried to tell me it was not happening, but total deliverance came during the St. John's Crusade at the Faith Temple, when the anointing of the Holy Spirit broke the bondages of anger, fear, cultic practices and physical bondages. I praise and thank God for his deliverance power through the Word of God. I thank God for sending Sister Pauline for such a time as this. I have a better understanding of my authority in Christ and with God's help will never be the same again. Amen!

133

ANALYSIS:

From this testimony, it is obvious that Macia's parents were religious people who were also active members of the Anglican Church. However, because they lacked knowledge of the Word of God, they decided to seek spiritual help from outside the church. They got involved in spiritism, another form of occultic devices.

They needed protection against the demonic attacks that could be coming from a relative who was involved in witchcraft. The innocent Macia then came under demonic interference through the protection that she received from her mother anytime she expressed fear. Unfortunately, her mother used another demonic method to pacify the demons from frightening those they have come to the house to protect.

Imagine, how can the serpent that deceived Adam and Eve in the Garden of Eden and caused the downfall of mankind, now turn around to provide protection to its victim? This is outrageous, an outright deception of Satan luring people into captivity. This parental indulgence caused Macia her mental health as well as her spiritual life, even after she had confessed Jesus Christ as Lord and Savior, and was also an active worker in the church.

Contamination by Birth

Just as it is in the case of parental indulgence, so it is with contamination by birth. It has come to the fore that some parents do make vows during child dedication to demonic gods or to a cult consulted during the early stages of a pregnancy. By this means, an unborn baby is sold into spiritual captivity. Thus an innocent child is dedicated to cults, in order to receive mysterious protection from powers and principalities of darkness in high places.

One may ask, how is this possible? Yes, this happens,

when parents are impatient for God to open their womb; when they begin to see themselves as barren or unfruitful; and all sorts of suggestions are welcomed. Women in this kind of predicament begin to go after fortunetellers, and divinations to seek means to produce children.

When a woman experiences delay in childbearing, she is tempted to consult oracles where many weird rituals are performed, to ensure that babies are born. As part of the rituals, concocted potions are mixed and given to a woman to drink; sometimes incisions are made in the private parts of the body; and satanic verses are given to one to read.

Note that any step taken during the search for fruitfulness or child delivery that is outside the Word of God is demonic. Any child born under similar circumstances is automatically initiated into a demonic world; a satanic covenant has been made; an impartation of evil communication is established; hence the unborn baby is already being held in the custody of powers and principalities of darkness.

It is clear that Satan tries to duplicate whatever God does, in order to deceive people. Dedication at conception is biblical if well handled with effectual, fervent prayers. In **1 Samuel 1:12-18**, Hannah prayed fervently for fruitfulness of her womb, after she had been called "barren." In her prayers, she made a vow to dedicate the child to God. And so she did immediately after the child Samuel was weaned. This manner of conceptual dedication is godly. It touches the heart of God. It has become a concept that people who have the fear of God have adopted. However, when similar dedication is made to any other than the Almighty God, there is likely to be a problem. The Lord said to Jeremiah in

Jeremiah 1:5,

Before I formed you in the womb I knew you;
Before you were born I sanctified you;
And I ordained you a prophet to the nations.

Zachariah, a priest, and Elizabeth his wife had resigned their hope for childbearing because of old age. One day the angel of the Lord appeared to Zachariah and gave him the good news of a great child to be born. Within the same season, a young virgin who had been engaged, but still faithful to her chastity was also pregnant with the Savior Jesus Christ through the power of the Holy Spirit.

The spectacular thing that is pertinent in the case of Elizabeth and Mary is the quality of their lives, as they were righteous and God-fearing. So many great events happened during their pregnancies. The Holy Spirit visited them on a regular basis. The presence of the Lord was constantly with them.

In some cases the unborn babies saluted each other to signify recognition of each other in the spiritual realm, as people with one accord, and with the Holy Spirit. The period of their pregnancy was a great moment of joy to the heavenly hosts, and to the saints on earth. Indeed, the Lord's hand was upon them to fulfill His plan and purpose on their lives from the time of conception.

Just like in the case of Hannah and her son Samuel, as well as Jeremiah, every child has an errand to fulfill on earth. It is either that a child is brought up to fulfill the godly errand from God the creator, or the child will be misled into the camp of Satan. A child is either privileged to use his talents and gifts to glorify the name of the Lord, or will be lured into the service of Satan. The training of a child depends a lot on parental care and involvement with the things of righteousness. The Word of God encourages parents to bring up a child in a way he should grow, so that he will not depart from the truth.

TESTIMONY OF SINCLAIR

My mother gave birth to me on the 4th of February 1938. Both my mother and my father played the coronet in the Salvation Army. I was told that my father was an excellent trumpeter. He was also a very good preacher.

During World War II, my father was stationed in various Islands of the Caribbean. After the war he returned home, then shortly after, we moved to Port of Spain, Trinidad. We lived there for two years. During this period, we went over to Tobago, where we stayed with a spiritualist, whom I understood was very good in her readings. The woman read occultic predictions as a fortuneteller.

My experience within that period that we stayed in San Fernando would make a good horror movie. During the early years of my life, I lived in constant fear—at nights I would see and hear things; there would be demon parties and music; we had no radio or gramophone, yet the music was there. I would hear people with foreign accents in the house. When I walked the road, spirits would call me by my name. Then my father became a Rosicrucian. I used to look at the pictures in his books. I can still remember those pictures.

By the age of 9 years, the spiritual harassment stopped. It was only on rare occasions that I would hear or see anything. By this time I had began to take interest in occultic activities. After I finished school, I spent two years learning a trade. During this period my father and I became close. He introduced me to the "Lemurian Fellowship." It is a meditation to the pre-Adamic age. I later broke away from them and joined the "Brotherhood of the White Temple," another meditation group, which gave me "power" to fly around at nights. After four years of intense study, I earned a certificate—Dr. of Philosophy, which gave me the authority to teach and practice what I was taught. I moved on to the "Order of Melchisedec" and "Metaphysics." I later fell out and then joined "Raja Yoga," a meditation group; again I fell out.

Then one day a friend came to my work place all excited, the devil sent him. "Come let's go and meet a woman who is an adept;" so I went to see this woman. I was drawn like a moth to the flame. Her name is Majori, not just a reader of occultic activities, but also an obeah woman (a witch doctor). I sensed she was to become my teacher. She gave me a bath, made something to bring me luck, finances, etc., and also worked on my marriage, which had started to go downhill. She also gave me something to drink to improve my health. The next step was some sort of initiation, but again the Lord stepped in and I fell out.

On Friday night to early Saturday morning in 1990, the Lord spoke to me. I did not hear a voice, but an instruction was placed in my mind to do certain things, which were unusual to me. It sounded as if the voice said, *"Enough is enough, stop, lend me an ear. Tomorrow bring to an end all this foolishness, and on the day following you must go to church, and meet my son."*

I got up that Saturday morning, burned all my metaphysic lessons; burned the certificate; *"Give me the strength to reach my office."* Also at night, something would come upon me, and I would feel as though they were putting little pins all over my body, as though they were making a cut in my skin. I burned all that Majori had given to me; burned my bed that I slept on; burned all the occult books; and Sunday morning went to church (Living Word Deliverance). No altar call was necessary. I knew what I had to do. I thank and appreciate the Lord for this deliverance.

Having repented, all hell broke loose in my life. Attack after attack came, but the Lord was always right beside me. I would be walking down Broad Street in Bridgetown, and all of a sudden, I would feel very weak. Then I would pray, *"Please Lord, don't let me pass out here."* I used to think that the Lord was too busy to pay any attention to me.

One evening shortly after I accepted Jesus as my Lord and Savior, the enemy attacked me. I felt as though I was going to die. He did something to the right side of my head. The thought came to me that I should call the Pastor, and ask him to pray for me. Another thought said you will have to become the Pastor's shadow, yet another thought came saying that I should run down the road and shout. But the last thought said, "Call on the Lord." I prayed, and while praying I was relieved.

I had to attend a training session in Dallas, Texas (1993). I said, "Lord you know that I will fail this time because the courses are compact; the time is very short. I cannot handle this program with the devil harassing me." The Lord restrained him from me. So during my entire stay, I didn't have any sort of harassment. I finished the course a day ahead of schedule.

A similar thing happened the following year when I attended a course in Antigua. I got involved in an intercessory prayer meeting that held between 4 to 7 a.m. throughout the period I was away. I met many pastors, prophets, evangelists, and teachers, but those who discerned my problems apparently could not handle it. Even some pastors accused me of seduction.

The first night I sat under the teachings of Evangelist Pauline Walley, I knew that the Lord would use her to deliver me. That Friday night in Oistens, Christ Church, I went to the church, did not feel like talking with anyone, or singing, or praying, just felt like sitting down. But as the Word came forth, all the pressures were lifted, and I began to feel good. I went home that night refreshed.

The following week I attended three nights, I was prayed for by Evangelist Pauline. She said that I needed to hear more of the teachings so she would pray for me during the coming week. I made sure that I attended all her teaching services at the Faith Temple in St. John Parish. For the first time, I saw signs of my deliverance. I wanted to vomit. I felt things were going out of my body, etc. This was the first ever since I got saved five years prior. Initially, the attack increased as I received prayer each night. The attacks came from every angle. I would be afraid to enter my own house after church, as the spirit of fear began to attack me. However, from her teachings, I learned to pray and to bind, etc. I also learned how to overcome the depression that had become a regular late-night visitor. Praise the Lord!

Sinclair's son, Andre Barker, who had also been involved in occultic teachings learned from his dad, refused to compromise with the new-found faith in Christ Jesus. He refused to listen or be prayed for by any of the ministers his dad ever came across. A night before his Dad's deliverance, the Lord gave a word of knowledge that someone's son was deeply involved in occultic readings. Mr. Sinclair Barkar owned up to it. He was then advised to bring Andre the next night.

I had a word with Andre and explained the implications of his indulgence. He agreed and surrendered his life to Jesus that night. After his renunciation Andre said to his Dad, *"Of all the preachers I have met, Evangelist Pauline is the only one I enjoyed and understood. I like the way she spoke; that was why I decided to give my life to the Lord Jesus."* Since then, Andre has been carrying his Bible around to read it at the least opportunity. Glory be to the Lord Most High who has made this possible. Amen.

141

Cultural and Traditional Beliefs

Every nation has its own cultural norms and traditional beliefs. Some are very beautiful, useful and helpful; such as the tradition of respect that is normally observed in the traditions of most African and Asian Countries. The people of Africa have a lot of similarities in their culture and traditions, such as respect for the elderly, parental consent to marriage rites and dowry, similarity of costume and the style of dressing.

Besides their beautiful traditional presentations, there are also some beliefs that contradict the Scriptures. These include the act of polygamy in marriage, which is fast eroding, as a result of evangelism.

Also in some parts of Asia, such as the country of Nepal, there is a tradition whereby three male children of the same parentage could be married to one woman. In this tradition, a teenage boy in a family has the right of a husband to the wife of his senior brother (with regards to sexual responsibilities), even as the senior man in the family does. Christianity is working hard on that tradition.

In some cultural settings, children are dedicated to the ancestors through the pouring of libations. Some are also dedicated to family gods or territorial gods (spirits) normally referred to as the spirits of the forefathers. There are some cultural dances that are demonic because they are specifically meant to invoke spirits (most often spirits of the dead).

Also, some of the highly celebrated festivals are actually festish ceremonies. In view of that, some of the special costumes, hair dressings and the general appearances attached to some of these festivals are demonic, and could bring spiritual contamination to people who admire and copy them as fashion vogue. (*See the next chapter on Material Captivity*).

It has been noted that the deliverance ministration for the individuals who have once been involved in festival celebration could be rough. Whenever the name of the festival concerned is mentioned, the individual manifests violently, some signs that depict the act of that festival. This gives clear evidence that the acts of some of the festivals highly celebrated are demonic.

For instance, the Crop-Over festival celebration in the Caribbean (especially Barbados) is not demonic in itself; the intention of its genesis was well intended and meaningful as being a time of rest from work (a vacation, a holiday), a time for family reunions and such. However, in recent times, some aspect of the festival has been contaminated with nudity. The expressions of the dance performed can best be described as an act of "sexual sin," that has perverted their traditional dance.

Similarly, the *"Sango"* (the god of Iron) or *"Oya"* dance in some parts of Western Nigeria, as well as the *"Voodoo"* dance (among some Ewes) of Ghana and Togo are strictly devilish, as this has to do with shrine worship. Human lives are often in danger whenever these idol worshippers are performing their *festish* rites (rituals).

Deuteronomy 18:9-14 says,

When you come into the land which the Lord your God is giving you, you shall not learn to follow the abominations of those nations. There shall not be found among you anyone who makes his son or his daughter pass through the fire, or <u>one who practices witchcraft, or a soothsayer, or one who interprets omens, or a sorcerer, or one who conjures spells, or a medium, or a spiritist, or one who calls up the dead.</u> For

all who do these things are an abomination to the Lord, and because of these abominations the Lord your God drives them out from before you. You shall be blameless before the Lord your God. For these nations, which you will dispossess, <u>listened to soothsayers and diviners</u>, but as for you, the Lord your God has not appointed such for you. The Lord your God will raise up for you a Prophet like me from your midst, from your brethren. Him you shall hear, according to all you desired of the Lord your God in Horeb in the day of the assembly, saying, "Let me not hear again the voice of the Lord my God, nor let me see this great fire anymore, lest I die." *[Underlining by author.]*

Effects of Indulgence

Leviticus 20:6-8; 27 says,

And the person who turns after mediums and familiar spirits, to prostitute himself with them, I will set My face against that person and cut him off from his people. Sanctify yourselves therefore, and be holy, for I am the Lord your God. And you shall keep My statutes, and perform them; I am the Lord who sanctifies you. ...*A man or a woman who is a medium, or who has familiar spirits, shall surely be put to death; they shall stone them with stones. Their blood shall be upon them.* [*Italics by author.*]

The twenty-seventh verse (in italics) reveals how grievous the sin of the practicing medium is before the Lord. When a Christian leaves the church and goes to the medium, such a one is comparing the power of the Holy Spirit with that of Satan. This grieves the Holy Spirit. Let this song be your guide to this warning:

> *Ye shall be Holy unto Me*
> *For I the Lord I'm Holy*
> *Ye shall be Holy unto Me*
> *For I the Lord I'm Holy*
> *Ye shall sanctify yourselves*
> *And be Holy, for I am Holy*
> *Ye shall sanctify yourselves*
> *And be Holy, for I am Holy*

Writer unknown

Whenever a person visits a medium, that person surrenders his/her soul to Satan through that medium or any of the spiritists consulted; then one's soul is held in captivity. From then on, one's soul is controlled and manipulated in the satanic realm. This kind of captivity affects one in the physical realm, as one will begin to yield to satanic activities unknowingly. So a visit to any occultic house or spiritual house is like a voluntary decision to hand oneself over to the police for detention, or surrender oneself into spiritual slavery.

1 Samuel 15:23 says,

For rebellion (*disobedience*) is as the sin of witchcraft, and stubbornness is as iniquity and idolatry. Because you have rejected

the word of the Lord He also has rejected you from being king.

Acts 13:6-11 records,

Now when they had gone through the Island to Paphos, they found a certain sorcerer, a false prophet, a Jew whose name was Bar-Jesus, who was with the proconsul, Sergius Paulus, an intelligent man. This man called for Barnabas and Saul and sought to hear the word of God...But Elymas the sorcerer withstood them, seeking to turn the proconsul away from the faith. Then Saul, who also is called Paul, filled with the Holy Spirit, looked intently at him and said, "O full of all deceit and all fraud, you son of the devil, you enemy of all righteousness, will you not cease perverting the straight ways of the Lord? And now, indeed, the hand of the Lord is upon you, and you shall be blind, not seeing the sun for a time." And immediately a dark mist fell on him, and he went around seeking someone to lead him by the hand.

The power of the spoken word is realized instantly.

Acts 13:12,

Then the proconsul believed, when he saw what had been done, being astonished at the teaching of the Lord.

A soul is won as result of the power of the spoken word.

Galatians 5:19-21,

...Now the works of the flesh are evident, which are adultery, fornication, uncleanness, licentiousness; Idolatry, sorcery, hatred, contentions, jealousies, outburst of wrath, selfish ambitions, dissensions, heresies...and the like, of which I tell you beforehand, just as I also told you in time past, that those who practice such things will not inherit the kingdom of God.

NEW AGE SPIRITUALITY

The New Age Movement of spirituality is the current mode of deceptive devices that the enemy has established to lure people into Satanism. It is a reception of all religious beliefs and Christianity, whereby every system of worship is believed to be directed to one God, but through different systems of application. This assumption is obviously deceptive, because the Holy Scripture says the Lord Jesus Christ is the way, the truth and the life, and that no one comes to the Father except by Me (Jesus Christ).

The New Age belief system tends to replace divine healing with natural health healing, and emphasizes healthy eating by concentration on herbs and vegetables. This ideology is rooted in the Eastern traditional religions, which are based on meditations and yoga—practices of Buddism, Hinduism, Martial Arts, etc. The practice of meditation and yoga are a sort of religious invocation to certain spirits that are contrary to Christianity.

The New Age belief also proclaims goodness to one another and emphasizes good relationships. This is purely deceptive as the goodness is extended to lesser creatures—insects and animals which they believe could be reincarnations of departed souls.

The New Age Movement also believes that everyone is a spirit and a god, and one can develop one's soul to become a spiritual "master" after death.

The New Agers promote astrology, emphasizing the use of birth dates and star signs to predict and dictate one's daily endeavor, future and lifestyle.

Testimony of Desaria's Involvement in New Age Spirituality

Desaria:

I had been suffering what was for me an inexplicable phenomenon for over ten years. I would struggle out of my sleep at nights fighting for breath. I felt as if I was being strangled. This went on for years. At first I assumed that it was some sort of circulatory and respiratory problem, something to do with the heart and lungs and lack of physical activities during sleep. After a while, I began to sense that it was something else, although I had never understood, nor believed in the existence of evil spirits.

One morning after living with this abnormality for years, I became extremely angry about it. I asked someone if he could help me. He advised me to see a certain lady who in his words "was good." My impression then, and now, is that he meant that she was a good person as well as knowledgeable.

This lady turned out to be a pharmacist who is also a spiritualist and medium consultant; who advocates natural healing. She prescribed healthy, sensible diets and said, "Take some supplements if needed, and do some exercises." But these obvious aids for a healthy physical, mental, even emotional person are mixed with other practices that are specifically forbidden in the Holy Bible. It is the masking of the forbidden with the good which deceives the unsuspecting or ignorant.

Let me state clearly that the people involved in New Age spirituality are convinced that they are doing good. The lady genuinely tried to help me. She spoke of the power of love and forgiveness, and gave me some prayers to recite. These prayers are very Christian sounding—prayers of protection, for self, family, love, light, etc. My only worry was that they were addressed to "the Masters"—about ten or so, including Jesus.

I felt very uneasy about directing my prayer through "the Masters." It worried me for days. Eventually I went to her and explained that I had always been taught that Jesus Christ is "the Master," and that I could not understand how he could be one of many. The spiritualist then assured me that this was so, that many have achieved the "master status" as a result of the spiritual quality of life they lived in their many incarnations.

I was still uneasy because reincarnation was a concept that I had never heard being explained in the church; and certain scriptures such as who John the Baptist really was had puzzled me. I must admit that this remained a worry for me. I realized that when I said the prayers, my spiritual oppression increased. Thus, whenever I used the spiritualist prayer, I felt a being entere me. It seemed bigger than me so I felt strange, as if I was being taken over. I would then call upon God the Father, Son and Holy Spirit, and this brought me relief. God used such situations to teach me the reality of what I did not know.

I was desperate. So she gave me some other prescription: "...bath with salt water; get a crucifix." I did not get the crucifix because they were out of stock, but got some "holy water." The night I used the prescription and prayed (and did not use her prayers), I had a lighted candle in my room; the next morning the candle residue was in the shape of our popular caricature of the devil with a harpoon and all that. Draw your own conclusions; I have drawn mine.

Eventually I discovered that all these experiences were due to an earlier involvement in the "New Age Movement" concept as well as participation in "Martial Arts," while my parents were also members of the "Lodge" society. I had an evangelical upbringing; therefore I knew the basic gospel message. I firmly believe in God the Father, Son and Holy Spirit. It is this belief in God's Omnipotence, and Jesus Christ as the Lord and Savior that must have delivered me from destruction; I am sure.

I prayed to God myself, and whenever I use the spiritualist prayers, I always told God that I had no desire to dishonor Him and to please show me if I was wrong. Space will not allow me to go into the things God did show me, except to say that the spiritual oppression increased enormously.

Sometimes I felt as though someone unseen was sexually interfering with me at night. But to me this seemed so far-fetched that I could not believe it. Yet the spiritualist confirmed it. For years my life had taken a downward trend. I had started a course of study in journalism, in which I was passionately interested, but dropped out after the first semester. I felt as if I would go crazy if I continued. After a while I could not even read a paragraph in a book without falling asleep. It was as if I was programmed to react like that. I felt totally unable to pursue my career interest in journalism.

I used to write poetry. It stopped. I had started painting; that also stopped. My back became so painful that although I was in my thirties, I felt old. I went through a bout of anorexia. The final straw came when I was informed that I needed radical surgery. The thought of surgery terrified me and it was this that got me on my knees, seeking the Lord.

Eventually one day, when it was particularly severe, I simply said aloud that I did not care what happened, I believe in God Almighty, and in Jesus Christ the Son of God. I believe that He died for my sins.

Immediately, the heavy oppression left me. And I repented of my sins.

It was at this point that Evangelist. Pauline visited my church, Abundant Life Assembly. I went forward for rededication and visited her the next day. I felt that she understood when I spoke to her. No one else seemed to. Her teaching has helped me enormously; helped me to understand more of what happened and to trust God more. She also confirmed what I had felt that this is not just of relevance to the unsaved, but that it is of vital importance to the Church.

With the permission of my pastor, she took time off to minister to me at Faith Temple, the process during which I manifested the existence of evil spirits in my life terribly. I was delivered from the spirit of depression, water spirit, serpentine spirit, Rosicrucianism, martialism, occultism, astrology, crystalism, mediumnism, herbalism and fear of the devil. I thank God for my deliverance so far. It is not by might nor by (*any human*) power; but by My Spirit, says the Lord. Therefore to God be the glory; great things He has done. Amen.

Poetic Expression Five

WAR AGAINST PHYSICAL CAPTIVITY

War against physical captivity
Humility is mine
Arrogance shall not be my friend
Submissiveness is mine
Pride shall not rule my life
My tongue shall be tamed
Indeed I shall be victorious
For the Lord is my strength.

War against physical captivity
Disgrace is not mine
I shall not submit to sexual sin
Lust is not my friend
I shall not assault anyone
For rape and adultery are shameful
Indeed I shall be pure
For the Lord is my strength.

War against physical captivity
Hatred is a demon
Envy is a companion of murder
Jealousy is his brother
I shall no longer strive
That anger may not prevail
Indeed I shall be sanctified
For the Lord is my strength.

War against physical captivity
I shall be sensitive to the Holy Spirit
The works of the flesh shall not control me
I shall endure longsuffering

153

I shall tolerate others
I shall love and make peace
Indeed I shall be Christ-like
For the Lord is my strength.

Pauline Walley, November 1996

Chapter Five

PHYSICAL CAPTIVITY

Isaiah 61:1,

**...And the opening of the prison to those
who are bound...**

Physical captivity is one of the issues that needs urgent attention in every Christian's life if one must adhere to deliverance as stated in Isaiah 61:1. To be able to achieve total deliverance, there is need for one to make a conscious effort to walk out of the daily life issues that bother one. One must learn to consciously renounce the behavioral attitudes that are unpleasant in the sight of God. Some of these behavioral attitudes are purely the work of the flesh that affect our human relationships with regard to tolerance, endurance and acceptance. The explanation of what physical captivity means will open our eyes to some of the main reasons a Christian may need deliverance.

WHAT IS PHYSICAL CAPTIVITY?

Physical captivity is the stronghold of the works of the flesh on a person's life, such as in character, behavior and attitude. It is a situation in which a person finds it difficult to control the behavioral attitude that is contrary to the Spirit of God.

A person held in physical captivity often takes delight in the pleasures of this world, as well as the lust of the flesh. Such a person is not willing to submit his/her desires for anything. Such a one hates to be corrected and could be unteachable. Such a one does not want to submit to authority and is self-conscious, easily offended, irritated, and does not admit the truth. Such a person often puts self-satisfaction first, and lives with complacency, self-centeredness, and self-righteousness; yet is very religious.

Matthew18:9 says,

Woe to the world because of offenses. For offense must come, but woe to that man by whom the offense comes! And if your hand or foot causes you to sin, cut it off and cast it from you. It is better for you to enter into life lame or maimed, rather than having two hands or two feet, to be cast into the everlasting fire. And if your eye causes you to sin, pluck it out and cast it from you. It is better for you to enter into life with one eye, rather than having two eyes, to be cast into hell fire.

CHARACTERISTICS OF A PERSON IN PHYSICAL CAPTIVITY

When a person is held in physical captivity, the one's character, behavior and attitude are affected. A person's habitual character is the strong link through which the enemy carries out his operation. Habitual character that reflects satanic strongholds in humans are identified in the book of **Galatians 5:16-21,**

> **I say then: Walk in the Spirit, and you shall not fulfill the lust of the flesh. For the flesh lusts against the Spirit, and the Spirit against the flesh, and these are contrary to one another, so that you do not do the things that you wish. But if you are led by the Spirit, you are not under the law. Now the works of the flesh are evident, which are: adultery, fornications, uncleanness, lewdness, idolatry, sorcery, hatred, contentions, jealousies, outbursts of wrath, selfish ambitions, dissensions, heresies, envy, murders, drunkenness, revelries, and the like; of which I tell you beforehand, just as I also told you in time past, that those who practice such things will not inherit the kingdom of God.**

Also 1 Corinthians 6:9-11 says,

> **Do you not know that the unrighteous will not inherit the kingdom of God? Do not be deceived. Neither fornicators, nor idolaters, nor adulterers, nor homosexuals, nor sodomites; nor thieves, nor covetous**

nor drunkards, nor revilers, nor extortionist will inherit the kingdom of God. And such were some of you. But you were washed, but you were sanctified, but you were justified in the name of the Lord Jesus and by the Spirit of our God.

SEXUAL SIN

Sexual sin is any sexual affair that is performed outside marriage, or with anyone to whom one is not married. It also includes sexual abuse whereby one performs the sexual act in any form other than the way and manner that God ordained for the married.

Modern day sexual perversion includes nudity, pornography, oral sex, and Internet sex, which could be classified as uncleanness. Anyone who claims to be a Christian, having the character of the Lord Jesus Christ should not in any measure be involved in sexual sin of any kind. The Christian life is a life of purity and holiness that contains the presence of the Holy Spirit. A Christian body is the dwelling place of the living God as recorded in

1 Corinthians 6:17-20,

But he who is joined to the Lord is one spirit with Him. Flee sexual immorality. Every sin that a man does is outside the body, but he who commits sexual immorality sins against his own body. Or do you not know that your body is the temple of the Holy Spirit who is in you, whom you have from God, and you are not your own? For you were bought at a price; therefore

glorify God in your body and in your spirit, which are God's.

1 Corinthians 5:9-13 says,

I wrote to you in my epistle not to keep company with the sexually immoral people. Yet I certainly did not mean with the sexually immoral people of this world, or with the covetous, or extortioners, or idolaters, since then you would need to go out of the world. But now I have written to you not to keep company with anyone named a brother, who is sexually immoral, or covetous, or an idolater, or a reviler, or a drunkard, or an extortioner, not even to eat with such a person... Therefore put away from yourselves the evil person.

ADULTERY

Adultery is any extra-marital affair that attracts sexual intercourse outside marriage. It is an act of sexual unfaithfulness from a man or woman who is married. Adultery is one of the sins that bruise the heart of God. It is one of the sins listed on the "tablets" of the Ten Commandments given to Moses and the children of Israel.

Exodus 20:14,

You shall not commit adultery.

Marital commitment to more than one woman (polygamy) is also an act of adultery. This is because God gave Adam only one woman for a wife. More so, when God considered the loneliness of the man Adam, he said "**I will make him a helper comparable to him**" Genesis 2:18. The emphasis here is one wife to each man. The Word of God describes the unity between the man and the woman as "**one flesh.**" When Adam saw Eve, he exclaimed, "**This is the bone of my bones and the flesh of my flesh; ...Therefore a man shall leave his father and mother and be joined to his wife, [not to his wives] and they shall become one flesh**" (**Genesis 2:21-24**). (*Brackets by author.*)

This implies that one man cannot be one flesh with two or more women, both in revealing his nakedness, and in submission to one another as required of husband and wife. You may ask, why did King David marry several women and acquire concubines? It was a result of the Israelites' demand for a King. The children of Israel rejected the rulership of judges and demanded that a king rule them like other nations. God warned them against the consequences, which they ignored. Some of the prices to be paid for their request included acquisition of wealth and wives by the king, which they consented to. This oath "unconsciously" led to David's adulterous life, which later affected his kingdom, and also corrupted the children of Israel (**1 Samuel 8:6-17**).

Individuals who indulge in sexual immorality and those who influence other persons to separate from their spouses may be contributing to breakdown of marriages. Such individuals may be attracting curses upon themselves and are liable to condemnation in the presence of God, unless they repent.

Revelation 2:20-22 says,

Nevertheless, I have a few things against you, because you allow that woman Jezebel, who calls herself a prophetess, to

teach and seduce My servants to commit sexual immorality and eat things sacrificed to idols. I gave her time to repent of her sexual immorality, and she did not repent. Indeed I will cast her into a sickbed, and those who commit adultery with her into great tribulation, unless they repent of their deeds.

APPLICATION

King David was a man whom God loved. He was described as a man after God's own heart. God gave David everything he wanted and asked for. However, when David committed adultery, God did not spare him. On realizing his sin, David repented and he was forgiven. However, in the case of Herodias (**Matthew 14:3**), who committed a similar sin, instead of repenting, she held the bitterness against John the Baptist for correcting her. This is because she was unteachable and felt too proud to repent because of her political position in the society. Hence she planned a revenge mission; so at the slightest opportunity, she killed the man of God to justify her adulterous lifestyle.

In the same vein, Jesus looked at the remorseful countenance of a woman who was caught in adultery, and said to her "Woman, where are your accusers? ...Neither do I condemn thee. Go and sin no more."

It is pertinent to note that God does not take delight in a person who indulges in adultery. However there is hope for the one who hears the Word of God and repents. In order for one not to grieve the Lord, please take note of the various verses quoted below and observe them. The Bible states that the sin of adultery is punishable by death.

Leviticus 20:10,

The man who commits adultery with another man's wife, he who commits adultery with his neighbor's wife, the adulterer and the adulteress shall surely be put to death. Anyone who commits adultery breaks the law of the Most High God,

Deuteronomy 5:18,

You shall not commit adultery.

And in Hosea 4:1-3 it is written,

Hear the word of the Lord, you children of Israel, for the Lord brings a charge against the inhabitants of the land, "There is no truth or mercy or knowledge of God in the land. By swearing and lying, killing and stealing and committing adultery, they break all restraint, with bloodshed upon bloodshed. Therefore the land will mourn; And everyone who dwells there will waste away with the beasts of the field and the birds of the air; even the fish of the sea will be taken away."

This is because adultery corrupts a nation, and brings plagues and poverty upon a nation as indicated in **Proverbs 29:3,**

Whoever loves wisdom makes his father rejoice, but a companion of harlots wastes his wealth.

FORNICATION

Fornication is the act of indulging in any relationship that attracts sexual intercourse, before marriage. The act of fornication includes living with a man or a woman that one is not married to (co-habitation); or raising children with a man to whom there is no marriage ties and obligations. The Word of God says such persons that practice fornication have no inheritance in God, except they desist from such an act and repent. The Scripture describes anyone who indulges in fornication as one with an evil heart.

Matthew 15:18-20 says,

But those things which proceed out of the mouth come from the heart, and they defile a man. For out of the heart proceed evil thoughts ...fornication...-These are the things which defile a man.

In modern day civilization, many are being discouraged from keeping their virginity. A virgin is being regarded as a "fool." There are cases where some parents have encouraged their children to indulge in sexual relationships, considering the act as a vogue. Teenage children sit down together with parents to watch and enjoy pornography films on video. Some of the films made available to children turn to portray virginity as "insanity." Teenage boys and girls in most "developed" countries now prefer to stay with their boyfriends and girlfriends rather than with their parents. They are proud to introduce their immoral relationships to their parents, who have also perverted their ways of life. Hence, this has caused a rise in sexual sin.

While holding revival meetings in the Caribbean, I noticed that most women were not married yet had children with different fathers. Teenage girls of about 18 years have two to three children. This is appalling. In fact it is always difficult to ask a woman, "Where is your husband?" Children are fond of making references such as "my mother's boyfriend," or "my father's girlfriend." This sort of act also encourages the children to bluntly refuse legal marriages, which they believe will hinder them from sexual indulgence with any man or woman that appeals to them at anytime.

HOMOSEXUALITY / LESBIANISM

It is the practice of sexual affairs with members of the same sex. When a man is sexually attracted to a fellow male, he is a homosexual, in the case of a woman being attracted to another woman, she is referred to as a lesbian.

Leviticus 18:22 says,

You shall not lie with a male as with a woman. It is an abomination.

Leviticus 20:13 says,

If a man lies with a male as he lies with a woman, both of them have committed an abomination. They shall surely be put to death. Their blood shall be upon them.

Romans 1:26-27 says,

For this reason God gave them up to vile passions. For even their women exchanged the natural use for what is against nature. Likewise also the men, leaving the natural use of the woman,

burned in their lust for one another, men with men committing what is shameful, and receiving in themselves the penalty of their error which was due.

SODOMY

It is a sort of dirty manner of performing sexual intercourse through the use of the anus (rectum). This is common among homosexuals and lesbians. Sodomy is one of the grievous sins that led to the destruction of Sodom and Gomorrah. The people of Sodom and Gomorrah were involved in sexual sin, and God could no longer tolerate the sinful pleasures that dominated and controlled the entire people of the city. The only judgment that could wipe out the abomination of these cities was consumption by fire. To this day, the term Sodom is synonymous with sexual atrocities performed by homosexuals and lesbians.

INCEST

This is sexual intercourse between close relatives.

Leviticus 20:11-17 says,

The man who lies with his father's wife has uncovered his father's nakedness; both of them shall surely be put to death. Their blood shall be upon them. If a man lies with his daughter in-law, both of them shall surely be put to death. They have committed perversion. Their blood shall be upon them...If a man marries a woman and her mother, it is wickedness. They shall be burned with fire, both he and they,

that there may be no wickedness among you...If a man takes his sister, his father's daughter (step-sister) or his mother's daughter, and sees her nakedness and she sees his nakedness, it is a wicked thing. And they shall be cut off in the sight of their people. He has uncovered his sister's nakedness. He shall bear his guilt.

UNCLEANNESS

It is a filthy manner of practicing sexual affairs between human beings and animals. In most parts of Europe, both men and woman are known to prefer animal pets as their life companion. Some lavish their desires and wealth on animal pets and treat such pets as human beings. They share their lives and properties with the animals, and call them by human names. They sleep with them on the same bed, eat with them in the same plate, and have sexual intercourse with them.

Individuals who practice beastiality do "WILL" their property (INHERITANCE) to such pets before they die. In order to protect marriages with beasts (animal pets), most European countries have enacted a law to protect the right of the animals to be treated as though they are human beings; and of course there is the "Animal Rights Society" in Britain and "ASPCA" in America.

"SNAKE ENTANGLES PREGNANT WOMAN"
(Weekend Nation: August 23, 1996, p. 14)

SAN DIEGO: Paramedics sawed off the head of a family's pet python after the nine-foot snake coiled itself around a pregnant woman's stomach and entangled her husband as well. Mary Anne Carter, who is eight months pregnant, woke up about 10 a.m. to find Calena, a Burmese python wrapped around her stomach and biting her buttocks, said police spokesman Bill Robinson. Her husband, Brad, tried to free her using a small knife, but he too became ensnared. "It totally locked up the right side of my body," Brad Carter said. Then a police officer joined in. No luck. "We used a crowbar to try to get its mouth off her. We had a good 15-minute struggle. It was two grown men and we were getting nowhere."

Paramedics finally used a hacksaw to remove the animal's head and release its grip, Robinson said. (AP)

How could anybody keep a serpent as a pet? Certainly, God has put enmity between the serpent and the woman. Indeed, the reality of the Word of God is clearly demonstrated by the act of the serpent.

Dog mess(age)! (Ibid., *Weekend Nation*)

LONDON: London dog-lovers who let their pets foul the streets are being targeted by a cinema advertisement campaign showing a man defecating on the pavement. The inner-London borough of Islington said yesterday it planned to run an advertisement showing a middle-aged man dressed in pajamas squatting down and fouling the pavement. "You wouldn't. Don't let your dog" is the message, as the man's neighbor slips on the mess. (Reuter)

Guess why a middleaged man wearing pajamas should be the appropriate image to carry the message across. Pet owners may go to court over it; and spend their fortune against the decision. Watch out.

Leviticus 20:15 says,

If a man mates with an animal, he shall surely be put to death, and you shall kill the animal. If a woman approaches any animal and mates with it, you shall kill the woman and the animal. They shall surely be put to death. Their blood is upon them.

LICENTIOUSNESS / LEWDNESS / SENSUALITY

It is an expression of lustful and immoral desire toward the opposite sex or sometimes toward same gender (male or female). Licentiousness, lewdness and sensuality are a group of demons that attack individuals, and cause them to practice sexual flirtations without respect to the human body and importance of sex in marriage. This group of demons can attack anybody, single or married. It is the demon that causes the married to commit adultery and the single to commit fornication. It is the demon that influences incest, homosexuality and attracts other sexual sins into people's lives.

If you are single or married, and you do face constant temptations from the opposite sex, irrespective of your position; that means the spirit of lust is hovering around you, and you need to rebuke it and cast it out. If you rebuke it on your own and it persists, then you need to seek deliverance; otherwise you will face strong advancement from the opposite sex that you might not be able to resist anymore. You should also find out what is it about you that influences the lustful expressions made toward you, and work against it.

2 Timothy 2:22,

Flee also youthful lusts; but pursue righteousness, faith, love, and peace with those who call on the Lord out of a pure heart.

If you are naturally beautiful, and attractive, you cannot do anything about it, but to praise God for giving you the beauty; for everyone that God created is beautiful (**Genesis 1:31**). Like Esther, seek to win souls for Christ with your beauty. Ask God to cover you with His presence that convicts whenever you encounter sin; so that whoever sees you will love you with sincerity and not with lust.

The doctrine that prevents ladies from wearing makeup, or jewels to enhance beauty, but rather, demands ladies to wear tattered clothing, and to present a shabby appearance have not solved the problem of sexual sin. I have counseled ladies who wear a doctrinated appearance and yet were sexually assaulted, sometimes by the very makers and watchers of that law. A lady once said, "I decided to wear a haggard appearance, yet men don't stop making advances toward me."

There are mentally disabled men and women on the streets who claim to have been raped by normal persons. Sometimes men who just cannot control their passion for sex impregnate some of these mentally disabled persons. A professional man was once caught in an act with a woman who was mentally sick and homeless. The insane woman lives anywhere on the streets of London, yet a professional man performed the act with her.

Beloved, the solution is deliverance from the spirit of lust. Rebuke it before you leave your house every now and then. The more you talk about Jesus in your environment, the more the attack that you seem to face; but do not give up until the enemy has given up. There are cases when you have about two or more men proposing to one lady. There are also cases where a lady already engaged faces pressure from many more men hanging around, expecting her to pull out of the existing relationship. This is a state of confusion, and God is not the author of confusion.

Here, it is obvious that the spirit of lust may be interfering with the lady. She needs to check it out. The watching men will disappear or fall on their knees, but the genuine man will stay in love to keep the relationship. If you know who you are in the Lord, like Joseph "'the dreamer," you will fight the battle to the end.

Joseph fought his battle against the spirit of lust through to prison, just to retain his fellowship with God and retain his dreams to be what God said he would be. If you have a dream, then hold on to it, and seek your deliverance where you will find it. Amen.

IDOLATRY

Idolatry is the worship of man-made images turned into deity. Idolatry includes the worship of artistic works, carvings, statues like the one that represent the images of "0the Virgin Mary," a false image of Jesus, the crucifix, images of angels, etc. It is also an excessive devotion to any object, such as properties, gifts and talents or hero worship. Anything which you cherish and hold in high esteem besides God is an idol. Some people worship images made of gold, silver, and statute. They bow down to them and offer sacrifices of praise.

Exodus 10:3-5 says,

I am the Lord your God... You shall have no other gods before Me. You shall not make for yourself a carved image—any

likeness of anything that is in heaven above, or that is in the earth beneath, or that is in the water under the earth; you shall not bow down to them nor serve them. For I, the Lord your God, am a jealous God, visiting the iniquity of the fathers upon the children to the third and fourth generations of those who hate Me.

HATRED

It is a strong dislike toward another person. Hatred could cause one to exhibit a malicious judgment toward the victim. It could lead to murder and injustice. It is a destructive spirit that harbors devilish behavior. Cain killed his brother Abel as a result of hatred in his heart. Esau strove with his brother and hated him for life. Joseph's brothers hated him, and so they sold him into slavery.

Proverbs 26: 24-28 says,

He who hates, disguises with his lips, and lay up deceits within himself; When he speaks kindly, do not believe him, for there are seven abominations in his heart; Though his hatred is covered by deceit, his wickedness will be revealed before the assembly...A lying tongue hates those who are cursed by it, and a flattering tongue works ruin.

Following the behavior of Cain and Esau, God said to the children of Israel.

Leviticus 19:17,

You shall not hate your brother in your heart. You shall surely rebuke your neighbor, not bear sin because of him.

CONTENTIONS

A contentious person is one with the spirit of strife. A person with a contentious spirit argues over issues when not necessary. Such a one is often in dispute and disagreement with others. The contentious person also likes to compete with others, even in areas where one lacks the ability and appropriate knowledge. King Saul was a man with a contentious spirit. He argued with Samuel over the responsibilities attached to his position as the King of Israel. He believed that in his position, he should be qualified to perform the role of the priest; to offer sacrifice and burn incense in the house of the Lord. He also contended with the abilities of David, and strove with him unto death.

Titus 3:8-11 says,

...I want you to affirm constantly, that those who have believed in God should be careful to maintain good works. These things are good and profitable to men. But avoid foolish disputes, genealogies, contentions, and strivings about the law, for they are unprofitable and useless. Reject a divisive man after the first and second admonition, knowing that such a person is warped and sinning, being self-condemned.

Romans 12:18-21 says,

If it is possible, as much as depends on you, live peaceably with all men.

Beloved, do not avenge yourselves, but rather give place to wrath; for it is written, "Vengeance is Mine, I will repay, says the Lord." Therefore, "If your enemy hungers, feed him; if he thirsts, give him a drink; for in so doing you will heap coals of fire on his head." "Do not be overcome by evil, but overcome evil with good. "

ENVY

It is a covetous spirit that operates along with other evil elements such as jealousy, grudge, hatred, ill will and malice. It is not far fetched from contention. In fact, it is important to note that one of the spirits that destroyed King Saul's life was envy. He displayed his envy and hatred for David in the open. He attempted to kill David several times but failed. He had no abilities to sing and play the harp as David did under the unction of the Holy Spirit. He could not pray and praise the Lord the way David did. Yet he envied him, and plotted to kill David.

1 Timothy 6:4-7 Paul writes,

He is proud, knowing nothing, but is obsessed with disputes and arguments over words, from which come envy, strife, reviling, evil suspicions, useless wrangling of men of corrupt minds and destitute of the truth, who suppose that godliness is a means of gain. From such withdraw yourself. Now godliness with contentment is

great gain. For we brought nothing into this world, and it is certain we can carry nothing out.

SELFISH AMBITIONS

Selfish ambition is an act of putting oneself in a place of importance before God, and/or before others in any situation. A person that exhibits selfish ambition feels more important than others in every case; highly presents and considers self above others. Selfish ambitions contain other evils such as pride, ego, and self-centeredness. (See detailed discussion in my book, *Somebody Cares: ...cares for you, ...cares for me.*)

One of the issues that caused the downfall of Lucifer is pride. He wanted to be like God, and he ended up as the devil because of the arrogance in his heart. His selfish ambition gave him out and he lost his position. Selfish ambition and pride make up the true nature of Satan; powers and principalities of darkness in high places are controlling anyone who cherishes pride and ego.

King Saul had the opportunity to repent when Samuel approached him. His arrogance, the inability to submit in public before others, cost him his life and his kingdom. He was a man of ego. In the Old Testament book of Esther, Haman is an example of a selfish, ambitious person. He once made a boast to his friends about how important he was before the King and Queen Esther.

Esther 5:11-13 records,

Then Haman told them of his great riches, the multitude of his children, everything in which the king had promoted him, and how he had advanced him above the

officials and servants of the king. Moreover
**Haman said, "Besides, Queen Esther
invited no one but me to come in with the
king to the banquet that she prepared; and
tomorrow I am again invited by her, along
with the king. Yet all this avails me nothing,
so long as I see Mordecai the Jew sitting at
the king's gate."**

His arrogance saw him boasting once again in the presence
of the king and Queen Esther during a banquet. Having
boasted to his wife and friends the previous day, Haman was
so full of himself that all he could think of was himself, and
of course felt more important than the king. When his opinion was asked for, thinking highly of himself as a "god",
and supposing that, here comes an opportunity for him to
gain open support to destroy the Jews. He made such
suggestions with all dignity unto himself. Feeling so good in
his talks, but deceitful in his heart, burning with hatred for
Esther and her people, little did Haman know that the secret
of his plot had been unveiled, and his devilish plans turned
against him.

Esther 6:6-12 records,

**So Haman came in, and the king asked
him, "What shall be done for the man
whom the king delights to honor?" Now
Haman thought in his heart, "Whom
would the king delight to honor more than
me?" And Haman answered the king,
"For the man whom the king delights to
honor, let a royal robe be brought which
the king has worn, and a horse on which
the king has ridden, which has a royal**

crest placed on its head. Then let this robe and horse be delivered to the hand of one of the king's most noble princes, that he may array the man whom the king delights to honor. Then parade him on horseback through the city square, and proclaim before him," Thus shall it be done to the man whom the king delights to honor!" The king said to Haman, "Hurry, take the robe and the horse, as you have suggested, and do so for Mordecai the Jew who sits within the king's gate! Leave nothing undone of all that you have spoken."...Afterwards Mordecai went back to the king's gate. But Haman hurried to his house, mourning and with his head covered.

Indeed, the evil that Haman intended against the children of God was reversed against him. Certainly, *"Touch not my anointed, and do my prophet (children) no harm."* Do not plan any evil against anybody.

OUTBURST OF WRATH

An outburst of wrath is a stronger term for anger. It is a controlling spirit that attracts other evils such as murder, strife, impatience, irritation, resentfulness, fury, and provocation. Cain displayed all these attributes as a result of envy. He was irritated by the excellent performance of his brother Abel. The only way he could resolve his envy problem was to kill his brother, instead of exercising patience; thus, polishing up his shortcoming, he burst out wrathfully.

HERESY

Heresy is the act of uttering atheistic pronouncements against the Almighty God. It is a blasphemous or apostatical statement that offends the Spirit of the Living God.

MURDERS

Murder is a premeditated motive to kill another human being. There are so many behaviors that attract and contribute to murder. Such behaviors are on the same judgment scale as the act of backbiting, gossip, slander, false accusation, anger, strive, and envy.

PHYSICAL BONDAGE

Other aspects of physical bondage are failure, disappointment, and instability. Other manifestations of physical bondage include: Gossips, rumors, misinformation, missinterpretation, suspicion, imagination, and faultfinding. All such things that work against the plan of God for our lives are signs of captivity from which we need deliverance.

Revelation 21:7-8 says,

He who overcomes shall inherit all things, and I will be his God and he shall be My son. But the cowardly, unbelieving, abominable, murderers, sexually immoral, sorcerers, idolaters, and all liars shall have their part in the lake which burns with fire and brimstone, which is the second death.

Deliverance from physical captivity comes only when one:

- accepts challenge to identify the problem
- is willing to surrender
- cooperates with the Holy Spirit.

We need deliverance from the things that destroy our soul and condemn us to hell. Every work of the flesh is controlled by a principality of darkness and afflicted by a demon. Sometimes the demons move in groups. (See my book, *Pulling Down Satanic Strongholds* for details on demon groups.)

Poetic Expression Six

WAR AGAINST MATERIAL CAPTIVITY

War against material captivity
I shall be careful
Fashion shall not control me
I shall be contented
Money shall not deceive me
I shall be wise
The Lord shall supply my needs
And I shall not want.

War against material captivity
I shall be moderate
Material things shall not hold me bound
I shall have self-control
Worldliness shall not blindfold me
I shall be wise
The Lord shall reward me
And I shall not want.

War against material captivity
I surrender my desires
I shall seek first the kingdom of God
I shall not worry about tomorrow
Worldly acquisition shall not destroy my virtues
I surrender all to Him
The Lord is my provider
And I shall not want.

War against material captivity
That my soul shall be saved
If the birds of the air starve not
Why should I be afraid

If the lily of the valley thirsts not
Why should I beg for bread
The Lord is my Caretaker
And I shall not want.

Pauline Walley, November 1996.

Chapter Six

MATERIAL CAPTIVITY

Isaiah 61:1,

...To proclaim liberty to the captive...

Material captivity is the uncontrollable desire for worldly goods and material wealth. It is that type of mind that places personal belongings above all other things. It is the heart that treasures worldly possessions and considers them as highly important in life. It is the heart that idolizes worldly goods. Material captivity is the stronghold that controls the fashion world of vanity.

The stronghold of materialism is embedded in the consciousness of fashion vogue and trend. It is a high taste for material wealth. In modern spiritual warfare, the enemy begins to use material goods as a means of infiltrating people's lives. Contamination of fashion products at the source of manufacturing is now very common. Such contamination includes body creams, processed and canned foods, children's wear, cosmetics, animalistic designs, artistic impression, sculptures, cultural materials, and idolized items.

CONTAMINATION BY FOOD

Contamination of food at the source of production is one of the secret arms of the enemy in recent warfare. No matter how beautiful a food production industry's package may be, one must make it a habit to sanctify all edible items before consumption. You may ask, how is this possible? The Lord Jesus Christ was tested with food, when Satan said to Him in

Matthew 4:3-4,

If You are the Son of God, command that these stones become bread. But He answered and said, "It is written, 'Man shall not live by bread alone, but by every word that proceeds from the mouth of God.'"

This temptation could be based on the fact that Satan was aware of God's ability to provide. God provided for the daily bread of the children of Israel during their 40 years of wandering in the wilderness. Satan also had the knowledge that God sent the ravens to feed Elijah in the wilderness. Later Jesus Himself also proved that ability when He fed the five thousand with five loaves of bread and two fishes in the wilderness.

Note that the miracle of food was necessary in times of difficulties and absolute impossibility. The miracle of food was often in the wilderness where there is no provision at all. It is for the purpose of foiling Satan's attack that Jesus always prayed over the meals set before Him and gave thanks at the dining table. Note that Jesus Himself, the Son of God, is Lord over all things, yet He did not take the consumption of food for granted. His meals were sanctified at all times. Jesus also gave thanks over meals in order to show appreciation to God for the provision.

Matthew 6: 41 says,

And when He had taken the five loaves and the two fishes, He looked up to heaven, blessed and broke the loaves, and gave them to His disciples to set before them; and the two fishes He divided among them all.

During the process of releasing the children of Israel from the "House of Bondage," the Lord commanded Moses to pollute the waters in the land of Egypt, which also affected the fishes in

Exodus 7:19-22,

Then the Lord spoke to Moses, "Say to Aaron, Take your rod and stretch out your hand over the waters of Egypt, over their streams, over their rivers, over their ponds, and over all their pools of water, that they may become blood. And there shall be blood throughout all the land of Egypt, both in vessels of wood and vessels of stone." And Moses and Aaron did so, just as the Lord commanded. So he lifted up the rod and struck the waters that were in the river, in the sight of Pharaoh and in the sight of his servants. And all the waters that were in the river were turned to blood. The fish that were in the river died, the river stank, and the Egyptians could not drink the water of the river. So there was blood throughout all the land of Egypt. Then the magicians of Egypt did so

**with their enchantments; and Pharaoh's
heart grew hard...**

Just as the Scripture passage indicated that the magicians of
Egypt imitated the miracle that the Lord performed through
Moses, the enemy has been in the regular business of pollut-
ing some of the products being offered for sale on the
market. The Lord's command was to gain the attention of
the Egyptians and cause them to recognize and acknowledge the Almighty God. Satan, being a deceiver and a liar,
duplicates this, and uses it as an opportunity to infiltrate the
lives of innocent persons. In some parts of West Africa,
such as around the Republic of Togo and Benin, there are
some idol worshippers that make human sacrifices.

Oftentimes, some greedy individuals pick up the
animals (usually goats and fowls) that have been offered to
demonic gods/idols, and then take them to the market for
sale. This knowledge put many Christians off goat meat,
because they were not sure of the source of production. One
may wonder, why can't a Christian ignore the sacrifice and
just pray and eat? The fact is that the foods are offered for
evil purposes. The sacrifices are intended to transfer evil
from one victim to another.

Sometimes it is believed that an evil spell transferred
through animal sacrifice is the cause of misfortune, sickness
and disease, or frustration in a person's life; therefore
anyone who eats that sacrificial meat may be picking up the
curse placed on the sacrifice. For a Christian who is weak in
faith, such a person could be affected, because it is demonic
and there is a curse involved. Therefore, it is advisable to
abstain from eating such meats if one is sure that the source
of production is not pure. Apostle Paul spoke about the meat
offered to idols in

1 Corinthians 8,

...Therefore, concerning the eating of things offered to idols...There is not in everyone that knowledge; for some, with consciousness of the idol, until now eat it as a thing offered to an idol; and their conscience, being weak, is defiled...But beware lest somehow this liberty of yours become a stumbling block to those who are weak. For if anyone sees you who have knowledge eating in an idol's temple, will not the conscience of him who is weak be emboldened to eat those things offered to idols? And because of your knowledge shall the weak brother perish, for whom Christ died? ...Therefore, if food makes my brother stumble, I will never again eat meat, lest I make my brother stumble.

In "Malam-Atah" market in Accra, Ghana, a woman who had been known to be involved in the practice of witchcraft owned up to some of the evil spells cast on people through food contamination in the market. The woman confessed openly in the market that she is involved in a witchcraft coven that usually held meetings in the market at the dead of the night. And part of their agenda was to cast incurable sicknesses and diseases on prospective persons who are not part of their coven. The witches also interfere with edible materials by injecting devilish elements that are transferred unto buyers through food items and meats. Sometimes they inflict flies and other insects upon innocent people's wares; and also cause food items to go bad quickly. The witches are responsible for the increase of rodents in the market.

This sort of demonic impartation affects the sales and profits of innocent persons. When a witchcraft spell is cast upon food items, it is either the shop owner who suffers the consequences, or the consumer falls victim to the workers of iniquity. It is for such similar reasons that shop owners in different parts of the world, including the very big cities like London, Paris, and New York are involved in occultic indulgence. The purpose is to acquire power to wield off evil interferences. The very educated people are members of a "Lodge," "Freemasons" and other power-wielding occult societies.

In London, some shops (especially the Asian-owned ones) are sprayed with incense and "holy water." All these things are happening, because people are not just being superstitious, but they are trying to face the reality of the consequences that they suffer. While the unbeliever makes an effort to seek protection against demonic interference, Christians should not sit aloof and watch them in disbelief. It is time for Christians to stand up and wage war against workers of iniquity. Christians should learn to fast and pray, break bondages, pull down the strongholds of the enemy and reverse curses in order to succeed in the midst of sinners and workers of iniquity.

Psalm 1:1-3 says,

Blessed is the man who walks not in the counsel of the ungodly, nor stands in the path of sinners, nor sits in the seat of the scornful; But his delight is in the law of the Lord, and in His law he meditates day and night. He shall be like a tree planted by the rivers of water, that brings forth its fruit in its season, whose leaf also shall not wither; and whatever he does shall prosper.

If you seek the counsel of God, your marketing strategy both in sales and purchasing shall be directed by the Holy Spirit. It is for this purpose that the Lord has given us such gifts as the word of knowledge and discernment of spirits. When I was a young Christian, I did not know much about the gift of discernment of spirits. Yet I noticed that anytime I went to the market either on an errand or to purchase food items for myself, I would hear the Lord's direction, instructing me to avoid some particular shops and also some particular food items being sold by some persons. Any attempt made to disobey will earn me a negative reception from the shop owners against whom I have been warned not to approach.

At one time or the other, incidents have occurred where the reality of the Lord's instruction has been manifested for me to understand the level of God's protection over my soul. Ever since, I have learned to ask the Lord for direction when it comes to buying anything at all, either in the most sophisticated shop in big cities around the world, or in any traditional market.

MATERIAL WEALTH

On the aspect of material wealth, the enemy has held many captive. The astrologer has succeeded in capturing the world with Zodiac signs imprinted on clothing (such as T-shirts, jean trousers), jewels (chains, earrings, broaches, rings, anklets), and leatherwear (including belts and bags). It is pertinent to take a closer look at the various imprints that appear on the items displayed in shops and the markets. One must not purchase items with an imprint that is not clear or which interpretation is not known. It is dangerous.

Recently, some Christians discovered that some of the label imprints on some children's items read "dedicated to Satan." Some individuals have made open confession during television interviews in which they credited their wealth to occultic association. During one of my revival meetings in Barbados, I came across a lady who had a chain made out of wood with the "Scorpio" star sign imprinted on it. Once I pronounced the name of Jesus she fell down on the floor and became unconscious. Then I noticed the Scorpio sign staring at me, so I knew immediately that she was being held captive by the principality of horoscope, irrespective of the fact that she was an active member of a church. Later, I called her and explained to her that unless she took off the chain the enemy would not release her. Immediately, she gave it to me.

The next evening, when I commanded her release in the name of Jesus, immediately her soul responded with a cry. That same night she faced a confrontation when she got home. She gave the testimony the next day to confess her deliverance from bondage.

Between 1977 and 1978, during one of our Scripture Union (S.U.) Rallys at Oda Secondary School in Ghana, Rev. Alfred Nyamekye who was then the speaker, gave some revelations about the secret behind most of the garment industries in Paris (France) and New York. He mentioned the fact that some witches control the very popular fashion outfits that are frequently in vogue. Just around the same time, the Lord confirmed Rev. Alfred's statement in the Ghanaian national newspapers. A woman wearing a T-shirt with an inscription "Kiss me baby, I love you" was walking along "Makola Number Two" market in Accra (Ghana), when suddenly a mentally retarded man intercepted her, and forced a kiss out of her lips. The screaming woman unwillingly submitted, as the madman held strong to her and licked her mouth.

What else, the mentally retarded man was offering her the service she was advertising on her chest at that moment. That incident cautioned many Christians including myself. From that incident, I learned that I could win a soul for Jesus by wearing badges with scriptural or motivational inscription. I began to wear one that had "Jesus Saves" especially when I went out for street evangelism. The badge attracted attention, and I did win souls for the Lord, some of whom are now ministers of the Word. The Lord Jesus warns us in

Matthew 6:19-21,

Do not lay up for yourselves treasures on earth, where moth and rust destroy and where thieves break in and steal; but lay up for yourselves treasures in heaven, where neither moth nor rust destroys and where thieves do not break in and steal. For where your treasure is, there your heart will be also.

A typical example of a woman who was possessed and controlled by material wealth is Madam Shirles. Listen to her testimony.

TESTIMONY

Madam Shirles was a woman who had good taste for material wealth, and great passion for buying whatever she desired. Her wardrobe was packed with beautiful apparel purchased from the very expensive boutique in some of the great cities of Europe and America—London, Paris, New York, etc.!!! And of course, jewels, ornaments and home decorations were not spared from her expensive tastes and purchasing power. Like her looks and appearance attracted great investment, so did her home, stretching from the kitchen to the dining room, the restroom (toilet/bathroom) could be mistaken for her sitting room; this is for your imagination of who Madam Shirles used to be.

Madam Shirles' quest for high taste and the search for purchasing power got her into places that later shattered her life. And her soul was sold into slavery. A false prophet, who claimed to be a "Bishop" of a denominational group in South-West London, deceived her, got her into a blood covenant, and made some incisions on her body. This covenant attracted a lot of misfortune into Madam Shirles' life.

Demons began to visit her home and to play husband to her. The spirit husband took control of her life and home, as a real human husband would do. The demons crept into every bit of property she ever owned. They possessed and turned Madam Shirles' property into their abode, along with her personal body, soul and spirit. It was a terrible thing for Madam Shirles as they dominated her life.

In view of this demonic possession, any man who walked into her life could not stay longer than eight weeks. The spirit husband made the men uncomfortable and drove them away. Any effort made to get married was often shattered even when preparation reached the height of conclusion. Nothing seemed to work. Her life was bedeviled with failure. And life was rough and tough. She said, "I meet intelligent men but have no lasting relationship, it's as if someone pushes them out of the door with force."

No matter the sum of money she made in business, there was no room for accountability. Something evil was usurping her source of finance. Her beautiful appearance began to disappear as the problems led her into smoking and drinking. The father of her children hated and disliked her openly. Fear and fright crumbled her prosperity. Multitudes of problems that suddenly arrested her after the "Bishop's" incision drove her into places where she thought there could be possible solutions.

Friends took her to palmists, crystal ball readings, tarot card players, astrologers, gypsy women and all sorts of places where the demons increased the yoke of her suffering instead of granting her relief. Each time Madam Shirles went into a prayer meeting, the demons tormented and lashed her back as if to say "Stop betraying us." The lashing was so severe that it drew pain on her body and tears from her eyes while she groaned.

Shirles made several attempts to seek medical assistance for the back pain, but to no avail. In the midst of her suffering, Madam Shirles did not give up the search for deliverance. She nurtured the desire to discover the Great God, whom she often refers to as "my Father." During one of our prayer sessions, the Lord opened my eyes to see how much her properties have been possessed by demons. In fact, the Lord showed me some specific things that she had to dispossess in order to receive her deliverance. One such property was an expensive table made of "onyx (precious stone) and gold." The Lord specifically showed me the table and also told me that it was very expensive.

In order to avoid doubt and argument, I told Madam Shirles that she should ask the Lord to direct her as to the items that needed to go out of her home. She agreed and invited me to come over to her residence for prayer. While we were praying, I discovered the table that the Lord had showed me. The more I tried to avoid the table, the more I saw the dragon around it. So I took a closer look and discovered that the legs of the table were molded with gold and in the shape of dragon. Then the Lord opened my eyes to see the dragon hanging in the middle of the house and at Madam Shirles' back. The Lord also enabled me to see how much torment the dragons gave her. I saw the golden dragon lash her back with the tail. It was terrible to behold as Madam Shirles began to twist and groan in pain. At the same time, the Lord opened my eyes to see the torment. I then called Madam Shirles and explained the whole thing.

Surprisingly, she admitted and agreed that she had begun to feel that something was wrong with the table since

I prayed for her to see the things she needed to get rid of. It was a big task to do away with the onyx-golden table. It almost came alive as if it were a living thing rather than an artistic work. Having gotten it out of the house, there was also the need to ransack the wardrobe and get rid of her clothing that had animal imprints. It was then that Madam Shirles discovered that most of the expensive buttons on her clothing as well as the jewels and ornaments she cherished all had the mark of anti-Christ (the dragon).

Each time she got close to any item with the mark of the anti-Christ, she got a discomfort in her body, that was similar to the lash on her back. So the discomfort became a temporary sign that enabled her to discover the remnants of properties that the demons had possession of in the house.

Soon after the table had gone, the next session of prayer attracted the gifts of the Holy Spirit. Madam Shirles began to worship and praise God in a beautiful language (tongues). She also prophesied and received revelation, which was a confirmation of an issue at stake. Her looks and appearance changed so much that her old friends showed curiosity asking so many questions because they could hardly recognize her.

She has become quite an excited woman in the Lord Jesus Christ ever since; full of joy and peace in Christ Jesus our Savior and Deliverer. Deliverance from material bondage could bring great transformation into a person's life, as is in the case of Madam Shirles. Glory be to God.

Luke 12:13-21 records,

Then one from the crowd said to Him, "Teacher, tell my brother to divide the inheritance with me." But He said to him, "Man, who made Me a judge or an arbitrator over you?" And He said to them,

"Take heed and beware of covetousness, for one's life does not consist in the abundance of the things he possesses"...*(parable of the rich fool)***...***"And I will say to my soul, you have many goods laid up for many years, take your ease; eat, drink, and be merry." But God said to him, "You fool! This night your soul will be required of you; then whose will those things be which you have provided?" So is he who lays up treasure for himself, and is not rich toward God.**

This passage could be related to the experience of Tom Bunyan in *Pilgrim Progress*. There are occasions when people are forced to compromise their righteous desires for worldly pleasures. Worldly pleasures could be tempting, especially when one is faced with lack and financial difficulties. Many ministers of the gospel (Apostles, Prophets, Evangelists, Pastors and Teachers) are often in great need of material wealth. They often give all they have and are left with virtually nothing. Their families are humble and often poor, yet content with whatever is available to them. The Lord Jesus Christ as the Son of God practically faced a similar situation while on earth as an example to man. He said **"...foxes have their holes, the birds have their nests, but the Son of man has no where to lay His head..."**

It is pertinent to note that Jesus Christ deliberately did not want to bother with the cares of this world. He was on earth for a purpose, and He was just concerned about the salvation of man, and less of Himself. If he had wanted anything of a material nature, He would have gotten it. When there arose a need to pay taxes, He commanded one of the disciples (Peter) to go get a fish with the money in its mouth, and the tax collector was satisfied.

The Lord Jesus was and is that rich. He has power and authority over all things. Wealth is nothing to Him. Due to lack of knowledge, people who do not understand the qualities of endurance have questioned the idea behind Christianity and lack (poverty). Some think that "holiness" means "poverty," and so they would rather stay rich in the world and die as sinners. Lack of understanding of Scripture with regard to God's promises and prosperity for His children seems to hinder many Christians from seeking wealth. The fact that Satan tempted Jesus by offering him the pleasures of this world seems to have robbed many of the ability to accept prosperity as a blessing from God.

Matthew 4:8-10,

Again, the devil took Him up on an exceedingly high mountain, and showed Him all the kingdoms of the world and their glory. And he said to Him, "All these things I will give You if You will fall down and worship me." Then Jesus said to him, "Away with you, Satan! For it is written, `You shall worship the Lord your God, and Him only you shall serve.'"

In the original plan of creation, God set up the Garden of Eden and lavished it with wealth—material, spiritual and physical. The Garden of Eden had gold, silver, precious stones such as onyx and diamonds. In terms of food, there were various types of animals for meat, fishes in the rivers and birds. God made the Garden pleasant and beautiful for dwelling.

Mankind lost all these great privileges when he disobeyed God's Word. And so the curse of poverty was pronounced upon mankind as recorded in

Genesis 3:17-19,

Then to Adam He said, "Because you have heeded the voice of your wife, and have eaten from the tree of which I commanded you, saying, `You shall not eat of it': Cursed is the ground for your sake; In toil you shall eat of it all the days of your life. Both thorns and thistles it shall bring forth for you. And you shall eat the herb of the field. In the sweat of your face you shall eat bread till you return to the ground, for out of it you were taken; For dust you are, and to dust you shall return.

Although the sin of Adam and Eve attracted the curse of poverty, Almighty God, being merciful, has long revoked the curse from those who walk in obedience to His Word and will. In Deuteronomy 28 God gave mankind the conditions for blessings and curses. The Lord also promised to bless the descendants of Abraham. Abraham himself enjoyed riches and God's blessings before he died. God renewed the covenant of blessings with his children Isaac and Jacob (Israel) as He had promised to bless Abraham's descendants with a land flowing with "milk and honey."

King David, a descendant of Abraham, enjoyed great prosperity alongside his spiritual wealth. The Lord was moved to increase the wealth of blessings upon the family of David, when Solomon succeeded him.

In 1 Kings 3:11-14, we read,

Then God said to him, "Because you have asked this thing and have not asked long life for yourself, nor have asked riches for

yourself, nor have asked the lives of your enemies, but have asked for yourself understanding to discern justice, behold I have done according to your words; see, I have given you a wise and understanding heart, so that there has not been anyone like you before you, nor shall any like you arise after you. And I have also given you what you have not asked; both riches and honor, so that there shall not be anyone like you among the kings all your days. So if you walk in my ways, to keep my statutes and My commandments, as your father David walked, then I will lengthen your days.

Job also enjoyed the riches and prosperity of God. He went through a time of trial during which he lost almost every material and physical wealth he had acquired all his life. Yet, the trial did not take away his spiritual wealth in the Lord. Job's spiritual wealth was a great challenge to Satan. Satan could not imagine why a humble man like Job should be rich and wealthy, and yet maintain so close a relationship with all humility with God. Satan then decided to challenge Job's wealth. Satan went to God and asked for permission to afflict Job with poverty.

Satan attacked Job's faith in God. Yet Job would not allow his personal achievements or material loss to affect his righteousness. Satan lost the battle. He managed to touch Job's material resources and physical body, but couldn't touch his faith. Job was like a tree planted by the rivers of water, which neither natural disaster nor change in weather conditions could affect. He was deeply rooted in faith. Job's spiritual status carried him through the trial and so he gained restoration at the end of it all. His later days were greater than his former, because his spiritual wealth was far greater and stronger than the material and physical acquisitions in his life. That is why Apostle Paul could confidently say in

Philippians 4:19,

And my God shall supply all your need according to His riches in glory by Christ Jesus.

Note that the Lord has not called any of His children unto poverty. Poverty is a curse. It ought to be rejected. If you are in need and facing difficulties, speak out the Word and reverse the curse of poverty upon your life. Remind God about the promise of salvation. Declare your stand as a man who has confessed his sin and found solace in the redemption power of our Lord and Savior Jesus Christ.

Nail your poverty to the cross of Jesus by renouncing it. Turn to Deuteronomy 28 and begin to prophesy riches and prosperity into your personal life and that of your family. If it is possible, fast and pray for some days. The kingdom of God suffers violence, and the violent must take it by force. You must possess your possession in Christ Jesus with desperate actions. A desperate seeker seeks desperately. And a desperate fighter fights desperately.

Take your stand and reverse the various curses in your life since you have accepted Jesus Christ as your Lord and Savior. Behold, allow the old things to pass away, and let in the new things. No more should you put new wine into an old wineskin. Take your stand in Christ Jesus and separate yourself from the old wine culture.

1 Chronicles 4:9-10,

Now Jabez was more honorable than his
brothers, and his mother called his name
Jabez, saying "Because I bore him in pain.
And Jabez called on the God of Israel
saying, "Oh, that You would bless me
indeed, and enlarge my territory, that
Your hand would be with me, and that
You would keep me from evil, that I may
not cause pain!" So God granted him
what he requested.

This is one of the many comprehensive prayers for deliverance recorded in the Scriptures which one could use to
reverse curses and change one's situation for good.

ANALYSIS

And Jabez called on the God of Israel. Jabez, a man
described as a child of sorrow, realized that his life was
being held in bondage through the utterance of his mother
who was also under Satan's captivity. He felt that was not
right, because his situation was contrary to the plans of God
concerning his life. He decided to take an action against the
enemy. "Surely, I must be released from captivity. I can no
longer allow myself to continue in sorrow," he must have
thought. Jabez saw the need to call upon the Lord. He
acknowledged God, and appreciated Him as the Lord God
of Israel, his Creator and Deliverer. "Oh that You will bless
me indeed." Having recognized who God is, Jazeb began to
lay his petition before Him. He asked for blessings to
replace the life of sorrow and pain. He reminded God of the
promises that He had made to His forefathers through
Abraham, Isaac and Jacob.

Why should he continue to live in poverty when there is abundance of blessings upon his lineage? "No more poverty!" Jabez declared. "Good-bye to financial lack. I must taste this blessing that belongs to me." Abraham was very rich in livestock, in silver, and in gold. And the Lord God had also said to Abraham in

Genesis 12:2-3,

I will make you a great nation; I will bless you and make your name great; and you shall be a blessing. I will bless those who bless you, And I will curse him who curses you; And in you all the families of the earth shall be blessed.

Jabez's reaction to this promise was on this order, "If God has promised to bless me and make my name great, why then should I continue to suffer? I must certainly claim my blessings and be a child of joy and peace. From now onward, the whole world should no longer see me as a child of sorrow with a sorrowful name. My name is great among other names because the Lord has turned my sorrow into joy."

And enlarge my territory: Once again, Jabez explored the covenant promise and realized that he suffered lack and financial blessings. He reminded God that he needed wealth to make his life pleasant and comfortable.

I will make you a great nation: A great nation is a nation blessed with milk and honey, silver and gold, riches and success. Jabez saw the need to establish a great business venture. He saw the need to expand his business and expand his tentacles to other nations. He must have more than enough to give to others in need. He must be a blessing to other people. He must glorify God with joy and peace. He must worship the Lord with riches and prosperity.

That Your hand will be upon me: "Lord grant me your divine favor. Favor before men and women, before the young and the old, before the great and the small, before the rich and the poor."

That you will be with me always: Jabez continued to lay his petition before the Lord as he sought divine deliverance. The expression of his petition could be interpreted thusly, "O Lord that your presence will go before me by the pillar of cloud by day and by the pillar of fire by night; that you will lead and direct me in the path of righteousness; that any time I call upon You, You will answer and grant my request; that your glory will be revealed in all I think, speak or do."

And that You will keep me from evil: "O Lord, be my Shepherd, counsel and guide me that I will not be deceived by the evil one. Convict me of sin whenever I go wrong, and reprove me. Make me teachable and to accept correction, for you chastise those whom you love. Make Your desire my desire, and cause me to hunger and thirst after righteousness all the days of my life."

That I may not cause pain: "Teach me to endure and tolerate people—the known and the strangers. Teach me to love them and to accommodate them and to share your joy with them. Help me to encourage those in need and to pray and intercede for the lost ones. Make me an ambassador of your Word that my life will reflect the reality of salvation in Jesus Christ. It is my desire to be an example of the Lord Jesus Christ in behavior, attitude and character. Lord make me a joy in people's lives."

So God granted him what he requested: The Lord God is ever merciful. He is the Lord of Love. He is the only one who cares and never fails nor disappoints. He listened to Jabez's prayer. He saw the sincerity of his heart. Jabez was honest in his request. He did not hide anything from God. Neither did he pretend to be all right. He presented his desires just the way he felt. And behold, the Lord granted him the requests he made.

JEWELS AND ORNAMENTS

Many Christians are not too sure if it is proper to wear jewels or not. It has been a controversial issue around the world. Certain denominational churches do not allow their members to wear jewels of any sort (earring, necklace, ring, or bangle), not even the wedding ring is acceptable. Some people judge your level of Christianity by the appearance, and so if one has a jewel, one is totally condemned and rejected. Some base their reasons on the fact that Aaron carved an idol from the collection of jewelry worn by the children of Israel and presented same to them as their god; this action angered Moses and he broke the first set of the tablets on which God had written the Ten Commandments.

Exodus 32 reads,

Now when the people saw that Moses delayed coming down from the mountain, the people gathered together to Aaron, and said to him, "Come, make us gods that shall go before us; for as for this Moses, the man who brought us up out of the land of Egypt, we do not know what has become of him." And Aaron said to them, "Break off the golden earrings which are in the ears of your wives, your sons, and your daughters, and bring them to me." So all the people broke off the golden earrings, which were in their ears, and brought them to Aaron. And he received the gold from their hand, and he

> **fashioned it with an engraving tool, and made a molded calf. Then they said, "This is your god, O Israel, that brought you out of the land of Egypt!" ..."And the Lord said to Moses, "Go, get down! For your people whom you brought out of the land of Egypt have corrupted themselves. They have turned aside quickly out of the way which I commanded them..."**

The fact is that even if there were no gold available, Aaron would have used some other alternative products such as wood or clay to mold the calf. It was not the presence of the gold that attracted the corruption, it was the people who were stubborn and had consistently angered God. Disallowing people to wear golden ornaments is not the identity card that one needs to enter the kingdom of God. It is the cleansing of the spirit and soul that is necessary. The spirit and soul of the Israelites were far from being pure. They were impatient and lacked endurance for truth and sincerity (fruits of the spirit).

1 Peter 3:3-5 says,

> **Do not let your beauty be that outward adorning of arranging the hair, of wearing gold, or of putting on fine apparel; but let it be the hidden person of the heart, with the incorruptible ornament of a gentle and quiet spirit, which is very precious in the sight of God. For in this manner, in former times, the holy women who trusted in God also adorned themselves...**

This passage simply talks about moderation and encourages us to avoid excessive decoration of our bodies. It encourages us to concentrate on things that are spiritual, rather than on material wealth, which could easily attract temptation. I have seen people (men and women) who wear expensive clothing and yet condemn a person who wears simple ornaments, which are not gold. Some even go as far as qualifying one as an unbeliever whose soul is damned for hell because of a simple (cheap) earring.

This manner of approach to the gospel is unbiblical; no one should try to make a doctrine out of some other person's error. It is all right to tell people exactly what the Word of God says. But to claim that the Holy Scripture forbids us from wearing ornaments is totally out of place. It is not biblical. We must be careful not to add to or subtract from the Word of God.

In the country of Nigeria in West Africa and Jamaica in the West Indies where about 80 percent of Jamaicans are Nigerians (especially Ibos), Beryl Allen, 1993, p. 14, some class of people believe that wearing of jewelry is sinful. Many Christians do not pierce their ears. They do not accept wedding rings. Some will not associate or have any thing to do with jewelry and ornaments.

In fact, the behaviors of many people from these two communities are very similar. It is also in the same communities of Nigerians and Jamaicans that daylight robbery at gunpoint is eminent. Individuals who adorn themselves with excessive decoration of gold and precious ornaments fall victim to robbers. Some have lost their lives in the process, while some have suffered serious injury. Note that similar behaviors can be found in the drug-abused neighborhoods of the USA and some Spanish communities of South Bronx in New York.

These, some consider, as a warning to refrain from using precious jewels. Some Christians believe that it is better to abstain completely from decoration of jewelry, since the enemy has a vested interest in ornament, and it attracts the gunman to kill and destroy precious lives.

DOCTRINE AND SIN

With prayer and supplication, let us learn to identify the material things that are sinful and could be a loophole for the enemy to attack and penetrate our lives. This is not to encourage the wearing of gold or any ornament, but to draw our attention to the various doctrines that seem to have taken the place of the Holy Spirit in the churches. Note that gold in itself is not a sin. God created gold and the other precious stones. Right from the Garden of Eden, the Lord gave gold and precious stones to man as wealth. None of these caused the downfall of man, but the "food" and "fruit" from the forbidden "tree"—disobedience and twisting the Word of God to suit their condition, was the act of sin committed by Adam and Eve.

Despite the fact that mankind was driven from the presence of God for eating from the forbidden tree, mankind has not ceased from eating. Although people claim that the woman was the cause of the disobedience, men have not stopped marrying women, and if the sin was sex, married couples have not ceased making love. So why should we stop wearing jewels?

Remember that gold was among the gifts presented to the Lord Jesus Christ at birth. Remember that the wealth of Kings David and Solomon were measured in gold and silver. Remember that the wealth of a nation is measured by gold and silver. South Africa was under colonial rule until the early 1990's because of the wealth of that land in precious stones and crude oil. Many lives have been destroyed in that nation because of foreign domination and the fight for freedom for the origines to possess the wealth of the land.

Nelson Mandela was held in prison for about 30 years for the same interest of the Western world in the wealth of South Africa. Ghana formerly the Gold Coast, and Nigeria were once under the bondage of slave trade for several years because of their wealth and rich resources. Recently, some parts of Nigeria have suffered from human destruction because of the wealth of crude oil in the southeastern part of the country. Surprisingly, none of the "strict doctrinal Christians" has thought of telling the government to stop depending on the gold and the silver or the crude oil that attracted slavery, colonial rule and the destruction of human lives; none has suggested to the government to seek alternative means of taking care of the needs of the nation. Most often the wealth of a nation affects both the individuals as well as the denominational church body.

DISENTANGLEMENT FROM MATERIAL CAPTIVITY

In order to release yourself from material captivity, you will need to be honest with yourself, and carefully consider the things you idolize. Otherwise, you will end up more frustrated with doctrinal rules, which will rather hold you in bondage and let the enemy in to suppress you with fear. Check your purchasing power. Reconsider what you buy and the things you invest in regularly. Ensure that you are not acquiring things that you don't particularly need. Ensure that you are not wasting money. Ensure that your tithes and offerings are generously presented. Ensure that you support a missionary or an evangelist somewhere. Ensure that the needy persons around you are given some form of assistance. Also ensure that you are not a debtor. Check your taste and quality of things you buy. Also check the quantity available to you and level of usage.

What are the things you cherish? How do you feel when

people close to you touch the things that you cherish? Can you afford to give your last bit of wealth (money, silver or gold) to a ministry to save a soul, rather than for you to purchase an item that you cherish? Can you give your best to endure for the sake of another child of God or ministry? These are just some few clues to how you can disentangle yourself from material captivity. (See <u>Prayer for Deliverance</u> on the next page of *Legal Grounds*.)

Poetic Expression Seven

<u>I SHALL NOT HURT</u>

I shall not hurt
Why should my heart be broken?
When I have Jesus
Why should I be bitter?
When my Deliverer is near
Endurance is mine
I shall keep a pure heart
The Lord is my Savior.

I shall not hurt
Although the whole world hate me
Yet shall I not hurt
Although my best friends persecute me
Yet shall I not stumble
Although I am disappointed
Yet shall I love the more
The Lord is my Savior

I shall not hurt
Although failure comes
Yet shall I be encouraged
Although depression comes
Yet shall I overcome
Although weakness comes
Yet shall I be strong
The Lord is my Savior

I shall not hurt
I shall endure the times
I shall not hurt
I shall tolerate others

I shall not hurt
I shall love others
My patience shall be rewarded
The Lord is my Savior.

Pauline Walley, November 1996.

Chapter Seven

EMOTIONAL CAPTIVITY

The Broken-Hearted

Isaiah 61:1,

...He has sent me to heal the broken-hearted...

B roken-heartedness is an emotional captivity. The emotion is the place of sensitivity that responds to the presence of the Lord. The emotion is the part of human body that responds anything that is directed toward the heart. It is the place that response to joy, satisfaction and fulfillment as well as pain and sorrow. When a person is emotionally satisfied, the enemy is infuriated.

Broken-heartedness is one of the problems for which many people do need healing and deliverance ministration. Broken-heartedness is caused by failure, disappointment, hurt, bitterness, disgrace and shame. A broken-hearted person is often overwhelmed by dejection, depression, frustration and suppression. A broken-hearted person is often susceptible to hatred, envy and strife or rejection. Below is a testimony that illustrates the agony that a broken-hearted person suffers when under emotional captivity.

TESTIMONY

This is a piece written by an innocent teenage girl I met during one of my evangelical works around the Caribbean. This girl, Narito, was hurt as a result of the sin committed by her parents, which had literally made her a child of sorrow. Her heart was broken by the circumstances surrounding her birth and the environment in which she lived.

Hear her:

> My name is Narito. I am 14 years old. I was born in the Parish of Manchester. I used to live with my grandmother, grandfather, brother and sister. The reason I am at a "Girls Home" is that I used to steal to get attention from my grandmother, because to me it seemed like she preferred my sister and brother to me. My grandmother always told me that she was going to send me to a girls' home but I always laughed at her and said, "Me mommy, you are not going to send me to a girls home because you love me too much." And months passed and I continued to steal. Then at the end of September 1995, I was finally brought to a 'P.O.S' (Place of Safety).
>
> A "P.O.S" is where girls stay for a while in Jamaica when going to court. If the child goes to court and goes back home, that's good. But for those who go to court and don't go back home, they get transferred to a "girls' home" Like me, when I was going to court for 3 days, nobody came, so the Judge decided to give me F.P.O. (F.P.O is when you stay at the girls home till you are 18 years

old. If you are fortunate enough someone will adopt you.)

Well I got transferred to the "Musgrave Girls' Home" so that I could get the privilege to go to school and further my education. When you are in the girls' home you have a lot of rules and regulations: such as I have to wake up 4:00 or 5:00 a.m. and do my duties. And they are done at 6:00 a.m. the latest. And if I don't do my duty I won't get any breakfast or lunch money. And many mornings, I had to go to school without lunch money or breakfast. And they don't encourage you to hold up your head high. When they see you talking to a boy they say, "You soon breed" (meaning you will soon give birth to a baby).

They always judge me by the cover of my book, because I was always talking to boys. When I go to school and see mothers come around to see the teachers about their children, I feel so sad. This is because I wish I had a mother who could do same. But when I remembered that my mother went away for a good reason to further her education because she got pregnant when she was 16 years old, I don't blame her for going away.

Although she used to send me things at the girls home and she writes me letters, I did not hear from her for a long time. In the summer my grandmother came for me and brought me home for holidays. When I got home I felt very strange because everything had changed. For instance they adopted a little boy and paid a lot more attention to him than to me, so I felt like stealing again. I felt the pain of seeing her pay more attention to the adopted child, while I was left uncared for.

At this point, I started to look up for some of my old friends' telephone numbers. I always cried and said maybe my real home is at the "girl's home." I would have my friends to play with and talk to. Unfortunately, my sister was not there because she went off to college and my little brother was always playing with the little boy my grandmother had adopted.

It was so boring that I left before the holidays were over. When I came back, I brought some things for my friends and the staff and I hope to go back for the Christmas holiday, or someone will adopt me.

ANALYSIS

As young as Narito is, she has already come into contact with the spirit in charge of broken hearts. Narito suffers rejection. Although she lives with two other children of the same parentage, she has no one to talk to. She lacks parental care and attention. She feels sad and this has brought her some measure of hurt. Joy and love seem to be far away from her. What is more, her inability to cope with the spirit of rejection caused her to give in to stealing. She does not steal because she actually has a need, but she steals because she wants somebody to talk to her.

According to Narito, no one says anything to her until she has done something wrong. So it was better for her to behave negatively and get attention, rather than do well and stay by herself. It is important to note that Narito's situation was caused by a woman (her mother) who was involved in sexual sin in her early teenage years. By the age of 16 years, the young schoolgirl had given birth and become a premature mother of three in her teen years. This mishap brought sorrow and pain to another innocent girl who is a victim of circumstances—brought to the world to suffer from a broken heart.

The grandmother decided to put the blame on the innocent girl, as if she were the cause of the premature sexual indulgence (see *Physical Captivity*) that led to her birth. This little girl faces life with much difficulty. Every morning she walks 3 to 4 miles to school, most often without food. She is one of the very intelligent students in her school, despite her predicament.

Irrespective of her excellent academic brilliance, Narito still seeks attention by causing deliberate distraction in class. The teacher that introduced Narito to me said, "She sees me as her mother, and so I try my best to express love to her every day, talking to her and encouraging her to keep up her studies. Once she feels lonely, she will try to get my attention. I can understand what she is going through, and I have been praying for her to learn to overcome."

SOLUTION

- Introducing Narito to the Lord Jesus as the only Savior who can bring joy to her life is very crucial.

- Teaching her to pour out her heart before the Lord in prayer, like Jabez did in 1 Chronicles 4:10.

- Teaching her to depend on the Lord, instead of friends because friends will fail and disappoint, but Jesus is always there and is constant.

- Teaching her to learn forgiveness and not to hold anything against anybody, but allow Jesus to fight the battle of life on her behalf. It is also appropriate to make her understand the fact that she can only receive forgiveness for any sin she commits, when she forgives others.

The Scripture says in the Lord's Prayer, "forgive us our trespasses, as we forgive them that trespass against us." This is very important because many people find it difficult to forgive because they are hurting.

Meanwhile, the Lord Jesus also said our offering cannot be accepted if we do not have a pure heart toward one another. We need a good relationship with the people we can see with our naked eyes, and to be able to keep a better one with the Lord God that we cannot see with our naked eyes.

Teaching Narito to love both her mother and grandparents despite her predicament, and to make her understand that Satan and his powers and principalities of darkness influenced her predicament is imperative. The need for Narito to intercede for the salvation of their souls becomes critical. Narito must also be made to realize that broken-heartedness is of the devil, and that the more she entertains the hurting, the more the devil will cause her to be depressed and frustrated.

Therefore she should confess her joy and peace in Jesus. She should renounce the spirit of hurts, bitterness and hatred she feels against the members of her family. This is because the enemy deliberately caused her to be separated for destruction, but the Lord could turn her plight into a blessing, as it was in the case of "Joseph the dreamer" who was sold into slavery.

Narito must be encouraged to pray for and claim her prosperity in Christ Jesus. These are some of the tips that would bring healing to her. This is what her teacher began to apply to Narito's situation. Hence, she now has a sense of belonging and feels loved.

CAUSES OF A BROKEN HEART

Broken-heartedness is one of the major problems that is eating deeply into people's lives. It is a cankerworm that is common in relationships like marriages and friendships. It is a disease that has taken hold of both the believer in the denominational church and the unbeliever outside the church.

In every nation's territory, the powers and principalities that control emotional captivity have a form of grip on a particular set of people. The spirit of emotional captivity interferes with individuals' mind-set and controls their feelings about situations and other person's perception. Whenever insecurity creeps into a person's life, emotional captivity will have a hold on that person's life.

Broken-heartedness is usually caused by unfaithfulness, distrust, and inability to keep promises, vows or covenant.

It is also caused by lack of achievement—poverty, unfulfilled ambitions failure, or disappointment.

It is influenced by complexity—inferiority, superiority, distrust, marital breakdown.

It is caused by lack of communication—misunderstanding and misinterpretation.

It is influenced by lack of education and/or knowledge, ignorance, naiveté and such.

EUROPE

In Europe and the United States of America, the spirit of emotional captivity emerges in the form of loneliness and depression. People are easily hurt because there is a lack of endurance and tolerance. People seek solace in drinking, smoking and drugs in their fight against depression. Many also commit murder and/or suicide in an attempt to overcome hurt and broken-heartedness. Yet the problem remains unsolved, because broken-heartedness is a satanic force that seeks to destroy lives. Therefore the services of professional counselors, psychologists, and psychiatrists do not have much impact on the spiritual angle of the problems connected to depression, and frustration.

SOLUTION

There is a need for individuals to realize that Western development can never take the place of God in a person's life. Also, material development and political development, which have a strong impact on the economy, have no relation to the heavens. Therefore there is a need for an individual to make room for God, even where the political system seems to dictate the pace of religion and godliness in the society.

Where there is freedom of worship, worship must be placed far above traditions and man-made doctrines. The liberty of worship would then make room for fellowship and create love among the brethren. The freedom of interaction will flow freely and the spirit of loneliness will disappear. Europeans must understand that the culture of "strict privacy, each one for himself" attracts the spirit of loneliness. Shying away from your neighbors is refusing interaction. It is pride, and self-centeredness.

How do you intend to share the gospel with people with whom you cannot share pleasantries. Therefore, you need to relate to one another. Cigar and alcohol can never take the place of human companionship. Recently, the European media has discovered that youths in Europe are deeply involved in alcoholism and smoking. At the moment, Britain is seeking a solution to battling this evil among teenagers and young adults. Even in the palace youths have been caught in the act of smoking and drinking alcohol. In order to overcome loneliness in Europe, you must have a friend in Jesus Christ. He is the one you can always talk to. Pray to God to choose your human friends. He will give you someone who is compatible, and understanding, a man of His own heart. Marriage to a person chosen and appointed by the Holy Spirit is the answer for an adult. If you patiently wait on the Lord, He will give you the bone of your bone, and the flesh of your flesh. Amen...

CARIBBEAN

In the Caribbean, the history of slave trade is deeply connected to hurt and broken-heartedness. The spirit of suspicion and insecurity is very fertile in the lives of many. The genesis of these could be traced to the period when the slave masters incited workers against each other in order to undermine both their family system and original traditional systems.

This act of intimidation also encouraged favor-seekers to raise false accusations against one another in order to gain the attention and promotion of the plantation masters. Although slavery is said to have been abolished, the spirit of slavery is still very strong in most parts of the Caribbean.

Most blacks are still busy seeking the favor of plantation owners, who still have strong control over the nations, and the economy. While the Planters are busy making money, many blacks are busy nursing wounds of hurts and broken hearts.

SEXUAL SIN IN THE CAREBBEAN

The system of breeding strong and efficient farmers for trading purposes caused the breakdown of family life. Therefore, there is continued separation and divorce as well as sexual sin everywhere. It is as rampant in the Church, as it is with the unbeliever. Some "ministers" are guilty of it. Surprisingly, the people of the Caribbean seem not to have considered the fact that their ability to claim the right to life should as well be exercised, along with the right to marry and settle down with one spouse "for better or for worse...till death do us part." Many couples feel uncomfortable with each other, insecure and too sensitive to tolerate each other. As a result, many marriages do not last long. Some separate within a space of two to six months. Some even separate after 30 to 40 years of living together.

For instance, I met a woman (a grandmother) of 65 years who was seeking a divorce from a man with whom she had lived all the days of her life. Her children are married and they already have grandchildren. Her words "I don't love him any more...and I need some money to pay off my debt."

In another instance, a lady said, "I am the only one giving. I am yet to benefit from this marriage..." The excuses for divorce and separation are very flimsy and simply based on intolerance. This is because some Caribbean men are yet to wake up from the past, and yet to take over their responsibility as the head of the home and family.

While the women are busy seeking their welfare and taking over the helm of affairs in the home and the secular world, the Caribbean men are yet to reclaim the freedom of the mind from slavery. And of course the women hold on to single parentage, and decide what they want.

Also the dependence of a nation on tourism encourages sexual sin and hurts. Many of the tourists impregnate women they never intend to marry. So there are many children in the Caribbean who do not know their fathers. Neither do they know what it means to have a home. The male children have no example of a father that they could look up to as role models. They inherit broken homes, and they cleave to their mothers as though they were their wives. They lack boldness and are insecure.

INCEST IN THE CAREBBEAN

The lack of parental (paternal) identity could be one of the major causes of incest in the Caribbean. Almost every female I have come across in the Caribbean has a history of sexual abuse, the most common being incest. Some men rape and interfere with their own daughters at an early age of 2 to 3 years old. In other cases, it is blood relations such as brother to sister, mother to son, grandparents to grandchildren, cousins, uncles and aunties are all involved and guilty of sexual interferences. Stepfathers find it difficult to differentiate between their wives and their stepdaughters.

There are cases when a man takes up both mother and daughter, and so has children by both of them. A lady psychologist in Trinidad and Tobago attributed the cause of sexual abuse to drunkenness and broken homes. She however noted that even the well-learned men in the society who are supposed to be responsible are also involved. According to her, many of the cases she treats reveal that no section of the society is exempted. "Even some `noble persons' who claim to be devoted Christians are also guilty," she said.

Incest is therefore one of the root causes of broken hearts in the Caribbean. Unfortunately, the laws of each island favor divorce and separation. These encourage the men to leave their family for about a year, only to surface later with a divorce paper against the women.

THE CAUSE OF SEXUAL SIN

Exposure to blue films, pornographic materials, nudity and indecent dressing are some of the major causes of sexual sin. Sexual sin is controlled by principalities and powers of darkness. Therefore, any child who watches such films (irrespective of age) picks up the demon of sex.

Sooner or later, that child will indulge in one type or another of sexual sin.

Also, another loophole for sexual sin is caused by parents or adults who expose their nakedness before their children. The nakedness of an adult triggers the curiosity of a child. That child will later seek to experiment with whatever he or she has observed. From that point, the child begins to exhibit lustful desires. It has also been discovered that both actors—the participant and the victim of sexual abuse—have childhood histories of having been assaulted.

Whatever assault is suffered opens up a door for a demon to enter a person's life. Deliverance ministration is the major solution that can set one free from sexual assault. Counseling and frantic efforts are very important to get rid of the circle before too long; otherwise it goes on from one generation to another, as the spirit of lust is easily transmitted.

SOLUTION

The persons interviewed on this issue blamed the "Plantation Masters" for their sexual sins that have passed on from generation to generation. But the truth is if indeed you have been set free from slavery, then you must learn to walk and live like a free man. As a free man, you buy cars and build houses of your own. You travel abroad on holidays, and you participate in government and partisan politics. Why then have you not thought it wise to have a settled home and stick to your wives and families, as the plantation masters do? Why do you allow the tourists to come in and transfer their sexual demons unto your children? Why do you copy everything you see the masters do except to live in freedom?

It is no longer right for you to blame the "masters" for the error committed about 200-300 years ago. It is time for you to declare your stand as a free man, and resolve your life. Plan to have a settled home, and enjoy your family by overcoming trials and temptations. Strive to be like the Lord Jesus Christ in your character and relationships. Learn endurance and longsuffering. Believe God to change your situation for good.

Determine to overcome your weaknesses. Fight the battle of life with perseverance, and create a new environment for yourself. The Lord Jesus will see you through if you call upon Him to help you. Amen!!

CONSCIOUS EFFORT

It is time for the people of the Caribbean to declare war against sexual sin. It is time for them to identify their problems and work out positive solutions. It is time for the Church to cry out against the laws that favor divorce and separation. In fact there are so many single parents in the -churches with broken homes and hurts. It is time for the Church to protect the institution of marriage; otherwise, the purpose of salvation of souls will be defeated. It is time for the Caribbean churches to promote family reunion, by encouraging spouses to tolerate and endure one another.

It is also necessary to spend much time to teach the truth about the effect of divorce and separation as being ungodly. Another issue that the Church should consider is the nudity and indecent dressing of the people. Wearing "hot pants" (short knickers that exposes one's nakedness) outside the home, could encourage any lustful man to rape a child. Walking about halfnaked is making room for sexual attraction, which could also lead to sexual abuse. Of course that is why rape is rampant.

Let the parents teach their children to cover up their nakedness properly. Both the Church and parents should take time and teach their children the effect of sex and the end result of premarital sex. Parents should also endeavor to sensor the programs watched on television. It is the duty of the schools to include moral ethics in their academic curriculum, and teach them throughout the various levels of education.

BETRAYAL (THE JUDAS SPIRIT):

In the Caribbean, it is easy to go into a church and discover that both the minister in charge and the members are living in hurts and nursing broken hearts. This is because there have been cases where church denomination founders/owners (ministers) slander and libel other foreign ministers out of jealousy.

Sometimes visiting ministers from other Islands or nations (mostly blacks) are reported to immigration officers, and barred from entering an Island. Sometimes the motive of the "Judas" ministers is intended to gain governmental favor (Political ambition). Some ports of entry have long lists of ministers from other Islands who are not permitted to enter to do the work of God. Any minister who preaches against "satanic doctrines," or "compromise," or focuses on teachings against the "traditional habits" that are sinful is marked and frustrated to the point of giving up.

The behavior of Sanballat and Tobiah is very common in some of the Small Islands where the "ministers" who are supposed to encourage evangelism send letters round the Islands to discredit other ministers. For instance, there was a case where a minister encouraged the government of an Island to promulgate a law to prevent international evangelists and missionaries from coming into the Island to conduct any ministerial activities. Hence, preaching or praying by any foreign minister cannot be allowed without the government's permission. Preaching without governmental permission is illegal.

This sort of behavior allows the devil to creep into the church and destroy relationships among brethren, and of course, families could be divided over such ungodly matters. Class and sectionalization only serve to encourage division and discrimination.

SOLUTION

If you are a Christian or a "minister," and you are fond of listening to gossip and encouraging false accusation, then you are not working toward soul-winning and purification of the body of Christ. You need to repent. Note that there are thousands of unsaved souls in your neighborhood, whom you have not witnessed to nor made any attempt to lead to Christ. You are only hoping that the Holy Spirit will touch them and bring them into your church. Yet you spend your time listening to the counsel of the ungodly. You spend time to make telephone calls to other Islands in order to frustrate other visiting ministers. Be careful.

God did not call you to destroy the body of Christ, or any minister. Keep a pure heart. Forgive your offenders. Allow God to vindicate you, and judge your enemies. Remember that the Bible says not all who call upon the Lord shall enter the kingdom of heaven. However, we should allow the weeds to grow along with the wheat. In the process of venting your anger against one minister, you may be hindering thousands of souls from being saved. Be wise in your recommendations. Touch not the anointed of God. Stop the gossip. Stop the false accusations. It could lead you to hell if you do not repent.

UNITED STATES AND NORTH AMERICA

The struggle for "equality" between men and women, as well as the rising of racial discrimination between the black people of African descent and the whites has contributed to the alarming increase of broken-heartedness. The equality syndrome has encouraged men to neglect the responsibility that was originally assigned to them at the beginning of creation. The man is appointed the head of the family even as Christ is the head of the Church (body of Christ), while the woman is the helpmate. Whatever law gives a woman the authority to rule the home, and kick the man out, is satanic and destructive. Once a man is thrown out of his home by the aid of the law of the land, the home is broken, and the children of that wedlock become like a flock of sheep without a shepherd.

Since the divine appointed head is thrown out, the children lose and despise authority. They become alien to instructions, and hate correction. Most often children from broken homes are sensitive and touchy. The lack of fatherly love and a fatherly presence cause them to feel rejected. Many such children do not want to be pruned or corrected. This is because the mothers involved in broken relationships often treat their wards like husbands, especially in the case of an only child. It is serious when the child is a male.

In some cases, where separated partners have gone into other relationships, the children from the former relationships have often suffered incest and all sorts of sexual abuse. This has also contributed to broken hearts and hurts. Also, the loopholes created in governmental laws affecting marriage situations have encouraged broken homes. Since the laws now encourage separation of marriages and divorce instead of creating solutions to resolve differences between spouses, men and women now feel it is wise for them to marry same sex groups as in homosexuality and lesbianism.

Also, some individuals find consolation in marrying their animal pets (*Physical Captivity*). Recently, some Episcopal priests were accused of being involved in homosexuality in the United States. One such scandal was reported to have been committed on the altar (*The Weekend Nation,* Nov.1, 1996, p. 14, and Nov. 3, 1996, .p. 13A):

The so called "Priest," 60 year-old Andriess, and another Episcopal minister, paid a 23-year old Wasticlinio Barros, a Brazilian, thousands of dollars every month to serve as their homosexual playthings. Barros said that the priests often dressed in women's clothing and used obscene language while engaging in sadomasochistic sex acts…Barros contends that on arrival in New York he was paid to have sex with Andries and other priests.

During a public confession, one of the priests involved, Andries, said he lived with Jairo as "my companion" and they had sexual relations, although living arrangement was "in a nonpublic manner in deference to my daughter, who lived with me, and to the parish." Some of the shocking statements made by the priest caught in the act read, "After the two solemnized their relationship in church, Andries said he went into the hospital for surgery…

"Shocking as these photos must be to many people, that is as a result of showing something as private as sex in a public forum. I certainly never expected to see myself so portrayed. Nevertheless, it is important to note that two of the photos are of me alone and two of me with Jairo…

"I certainly unleashed Pandora's box. I repent of my sins. I now realize that I was used by two hustlers. While it is not pretty to acknowledge, it was self-deception to think that a relationship with a 33-year age gap could be truly mutual. Infatuation blinded

225

me to this reality. I chastise myself for
having allowed pictures to be taken of me in
bed with Jairo. I also chastise myself for not
destroying them."

This testimony is one of the results of broken homes,
where a nation or church condones sexual sin as in the day
of Sodom and Gomorrah. The families of these homosexual
men are bound to suffer broken-heartedness. This is an act
of shame and disgrace to both a nation, to the individual and
to the denominational organization involved. Many of the
persons associated with these men will also be affected.

SOLUTION

It is time for the individuals to differentiate between
infatuation, lust and sincere love. The spirit of lust and
deception is strongly interfering with many people in these
nations. Some of the churches are strongly affected. Suppose
believers now marry and divorce at will, and quote Scripture
passages to support their decisions. If a husband and a wife
can no longer live together, where is the place of God in their
lives? Note once again that anyone who kicks against the
institution of marriage without any justification, or to fulfill a
lustful passion will certainly end up in damnation.

The fruit of the Spirit is our identity card for acceptance
into the kingdom of God. And the fruit of the Spirit includes
love, longsuffering, endurance and self-control. The
believer's testimony is rooted in tribulation, perseverance,
character and hope **(Romans 5:3-5)**. A person can boast of
the presence of God and the infilling of the Holy Spirit in
one's life only if one remains steadfast in a long suffering.

If you are hurting because of lack of faithfulness and
honesty, then you need to fast and pray. How many times do
you fast and pray for your spouse and the success of your

marriage? How long ago did you intercede for your spouse regarding his/her character and behavior toward you and others? How long ago did you fast and pray over his/her business? What is your contribution toward your marriage—spiritually, materially, physically, financially, and emotionally? Are you always on the receiving end with high expectations, or are you on the giving end with murmuring and grumbling heart, and complaining as you give?

Check your motive and confess it, repent and forgive your partner. God is the rewarder of your services if you do it honestly and faithfully out of love. Why did you marry your spouse? Change your motive and get it right. Now, learn to understand your spouse.

Renounce every negative character you do not appreciate prayerfully. Pray the positive things of Scripture into his/her life. Pray the fear of God into his/her soul and spirit. Magnify the good things in his/her life. Admire him/her and appreciate the good things in his/her life. The Word of God says, "He who endures to the end shall overcome." Treat him/her like your son or daughter that you can never throw away. For no matter how bad your child is, you will still love and cherish that child. Your spouse is the bone of your bone and the flesh of your flesh. If you cannot cut off your hand or any part of your body because it is hurting or not functioning well, then you must not throw away your spouse for the same reason.

Work out your marriage with love, and save a place for yourself in the kingdom of God. Do not allow the counsel of the ungodly to deceive you and destroy your marriage. Note that not all lawmakers representing the nation have the fear of God. Some of the "noble" men involved in drafting the laws are Satanists (agents of the devil). That is why the Church must rise up and pray against the counsel of the ungodly.

Psalm 1:1-6 says,

Blessed is the man who walks not in the counsel of the ungodly, nor stands in the path of sinners, nor sits in the seat of the scornful; But his delight is in the Law of the Lord, and in His law he meditates day and night. He shall be like a tree planted by the rivers of water, that brings forth its fruit in its season, whose leaf also shall not wither, and whatever he does shall prosper. The ungodly are not so, but are like chaff which the wind drives away. Therefore the ungodly shall not stand in the judgment, or sinners in the congregation of the righteous. For the Lord knows the way of the righteous, But the way of the ungodly shall perish.

ANALYSIS:

This first chapter of the book of Psalms testifies to the fact that if you follow a man-made law or doctrine blindly, you will end up in damnation. This is why the Scriptures encourage us to pray for the government and the nations. God's anger could come upon a whole nation that is corrupted as happened during the time of Sodom and Gomorrah. Even the whole nation of Israel was released into captivity because of her sin. Therefore, God will not spare any person who compromises with the sin of a nation.

It is the duty of the Church to pray and cry against the laws that frustrate the Word of God. It is the duty of the Church to preserve the Word of God. It is the duty of the Church to expose what sin is and remind the people to resist it. It is the duty of the Church to instruct and correct the people that go wrong. If the Church neglects her duty to correct, the enemy will take over and control the lives of the people, as well as the homes. Both marriages and families will suffer as well as the individuals who have failed in their duties.

RACE AND COLOR

Racial discrimination gives a strong feeling of depression and rejection to the less privileged. Many have been killed while others have resorted to suicide because they could not cope with the tension and the hurts involved. The less privileged have resorted to drugs and crime as a defensive measure of protection. Unfortunately, the indulgence in crime has added more sorrow to the burden of the broken-hearted, as they resort to destruction of lives among themselves.

SOLUTION

There is a need for the Church of God and individual Christians to fight against any vogue or law that is ungodly. This is because if the Church keeps quiet, Satan will release his agents to rule the nations. It is the duty of the Church and individual Christians to war against immorality, and call the nation to discipline.

The Church must also call for moral education in institution of learning so that the young generation will not imbibe the bad behavior in the American society. The Church must speak out loudly, and rebuke the politicians and the persons who encourage sin and perversion. If the Church refuses to correct and direct the nation, corruption will have a grip on the people, and the Church will suffer for it, as her leaders will be hooked and stray from the gospel.

The greatest solution that America needs today, is to war against sin, and give open rebuke to defaulters of biblical truth. "In God We Trust"—let the trust in God be faithfully observed. Amen!!

AFRICA

Politics and poverty are the cause of hurts and broken hearts to many African nations. "Power-drunken" politicians, in an attempt to force their way up the ladder to gain their ambition, have brought sorrows to many individuals and families. Political opponents incite the poor and the neglected against each other, causing destruction of lives and properties. Massive destruction resulting from rioting that takes place during political campaign has contributed to the poverty line of each nation in the continent of Africa.

Although many African countries are blessed with riches and great resources such as Ghana for its Gold Coast, Nigeria for its crude oil, Sierra Leone for its diamonds, South Africa for diamonds; yet the West still has dominion over the wealth in Africa nations. Wherever natural resources abound, there is a sort of tribal and political dispute often incited by the Western nations. The West capitalizes on such disputes to portray Africa as the dark continent still living in a primitive era.

In some cases Africa is seen as one small country. In fact, in the Caribbean, many people including university graduates do not have the slightest idea that Africa is a continent with 52 countries. Neither do they know that Nigeria alone has a population of 120 million, while Ghana has 45 million people. Similarly, many people living in America think the United States is the world and other nations around the world are like cottages that depend on America for milk and honey.

CAUSES OF POVERTY

Every nation has a class of poor people that live in shanty houses, and slums. The United States of America has its shanties and the ghettos, as well as a poverty stricken set of people, some of whom are street beggars. Great Britain is no exemption either. Despite the system of income support, the taxation system still increases the burden of the poor, many of who now live behind prison bars.

From Western Europe, through North and South America and the Caribbean, there are poor people all over the world. Therefore, it is no strange thing to highlight the poverty of Africa in Western television media. The question is why are many nations of Africa poor materially, when they have all the rich mineral resources? This is because the Western world still has a strong control over the wealth that comes out of the continent of Africa. The West dictates the monetary system through the World Bank policy (devaluation of currencies).

Why the civil wars? It is still the West that produces the arms and also supports the national rebels. Some of the rebels are influenced by the manufacturers of the weapons. Sometimes the civil war could be influenced by pressure groups that want to have access to the wealth of some African nations. This is evident in the case of Liberia's civil war in West Africa, where some Western nations are said to be supporting the rebels with arms.

During the period of war, many people are destroyed along with material and financial property. A whole nation could be left in ruins. Civil war is demonic and ungodly. On the other hand, the traditional chieftaincy system seems to affect the political system, whereby leadership is appointed for life. However, this behavior is peculiar with greedy individuals who often handle the nation like personal property. The great promises made during election are soon forgotten as soon as the glory of leadership is tasted. Hence, the masses are oppressed, and the poor are made poorer while the rich get richer.

SOLUTION

There is a need for the body of Christ in each African nation to come together with one accord and pray specific prayers to uproot social evils often caused by political aspirants. There is also a need for the body of Christ to lead the nations in consistent intercessory prayer for the choice of leaders before and after election.

There is also a need to monitor the people at the helm of affairs on our knees, by praying specific prayers to change their motives and ungodly behavior. In fact, there is a need to pray for conviction of sin unto repentance to come upon all the politicians, members of parliament, the lawmakers and the leaders of the nations.

Churches should begin to pray violent prayers against interfering nations that have strong and subtle control over other nations. There is a need to pray against rebels and civil war as the spirits of darkness and greed. Pray against corruption and destruction of souls and national wealth. Break the stronghold of poverty, lack and financial crisis. Release the wealth of the nations from the hands of the West, and the rebels.

Release prosperity into every home and family. Let the words of the mouth over the nation be positive. Make special effort to bless your nation daily. Make effort to fast and pray for the leaders as well as the body of Christ. Let your song be "Africa shall be saved." Amen!!

SOCIAL EVILS

Broken hearts and hurts do encourage social evils. Where the law of a nation is unfavorable, the people who are frustrated resort to all sorts of mannerisms to seek governmental attention. In addition, politicians seeking the vote of the common man do incite the poor to commit atrocities, which cause national disruption. This is so because the politician's propaganda is often centered on the problems of the people. The politician therefore helps to create more problems, so that he can make great and enticing promises to resolve them.

For instance, the dejected souls of Jamaica reside in the inner city of Kingston. This set of people is known as the rejected and frustrated. However, they are the creative set of people whose imaginations are expressed in lyrics. Their burdens, hurts and lifestyle are reflected in the songs they compose. These songs are carried through all available means of communication systems across the world. The detailed lyrics of the reggae music are written by broken-hearted persons seeking identity.

The politicians capitalize on the existing problems, and distribute guns among them to kill each other ("gun-crop"). Of course the Western media finds this very interesting and newsworthy, and give Jamaica a negative coverage from this point of view. The identity crisis among this dejected set of people gave birth to the dreadlocks and Rastafarianism.

The longing to belong, and the desire to be identified is so strong among this set of broken-hearted. Unfortunately, the dreadlocks hairstyle, which emanated from the slums of Jamaica is mistaken for the image of Jamaica and also the root of black people from Africa.

Please note that Africans are not dirty and do not wear dreadlocks. The set of people that wear dreadlocks in some parts of Africa are the demon-possessed or the mentally retarded, and it is also the mark of some idol worshippers. The set of Jamaicans that wear the dreadlocks are Rastafarians, the Jah worshippers. Rastafarianism is demonic and is not African at all. Most Africans are God-fearing people, neat and beautiful. The men's hair are neatly trimmed or shaven, while the ladies' hair is beautifully plaited or braided.

It is only the mentally retarded individual who leaves his hair in dirty dreadlocks. However, people seeking identity to heal their broken hearts have resorted to all sorts of appearances, and weird-looking fashion vogue to console themselves (*Physical Captivity*). Every mistake is a new fashion style.

HEALING THE BROKEN-HEARTED

There is one major solution to the problem of the broken-hearted. First, you must identify the root cause of your problem: why is your heart broken, or why are you hurt? Otherwise, it will be difficult to get the solution. For instance, if you are prone to sexual assault like rape, incest, fornication, and adultery—then you must check your dressing—what kind of dress do you often wear? What were you wearing at the time of the assault? Check your attitude toward men. How long have you known the man who assaulted you? What is your relationship with him? If he is your husband, then he didn't rape you, the two of you just have to understand each other. What kind of conversation transpires between the two of you? Have you ever tried to resist him? Have you ever reported his advancement to somebody who could intervene?

INCEST

In the African society, although traditional beliefs differ from nation to nation, incest is generally an unpardonable sexual sin. Persons caught in the act of incest can be ostracized or banished from the society or from his neighborhood. Otherwise, one will be forced to marry the victim in order to remove shame and the consequences involved. However, incest is an abomination that attracts curses upon the life of the practitioner.

If a biologically related individual has been trying to interfere with you, have you ever mentioned it to your parents? If it is your own parent, have you ever told your teacher in school or pastor in the church or called for the social welfare or the police? In checking out the root cause of sexual abuse, try to be faithful to examine your personal desire toward the opposite gender; otherwise, no one can help you out.

Secondly, after you have discovered the root cause, then work out the solution to uproot it. In the case of sexual abuse, if you are beautiful and attractive, then begin to wear the type of clothing that will not reveal or expose the sensitive parts of your body. If you intend to wear shorts, then make sure your thighs are covered. If trousers or pants, then make them loose, if too tight, you will be passing a message on to a lustful person. If your skirt is too short, it will be easy for a man to tear it off and have a lustful time with you. Change the pattern of your dressing and appear responsible. The opposite sex will respect you.

Thirdly, bear in mind that the mango tree has the ability to spring forth again and blossom if its branches or stem are cut off, and the root is not destroyed by fire. Therefore do not handle your own problem shabbily, nor should you put blame on anybody for your predicament. Just make every possible effort to uproot the cause from your life.

Confess your personal contribution to that sin that broke your heart, and repent. Forgive all the parties involved. Release them and then forgive yourself and release your spirit by surrendering to God. If you do this diligently, then you will be free for good.

POVERTY

If you are broken-hearted because of lack of finances or general poverty, then examine your potential gifts and talents. Work out the possibility of exploiting one of your abilities. Do not dabble in too many things at a time. Try to do one thing at a time. For instance, if you are good at cooking, well then, try to help somebody with cooking. That person may recommend you to a restaurant. Or, if you can roast peanuts, then buy a small portion of nuts, roast them, and put them in small bags and try to sell them for a reasonable price. Go stand by a park or a busy intersection/junction and offer them for sale.

Pray that the Lord will release mercy and favor upon your peanuts. Bless the people who price or buy. They will return and ask for you. Keep a good countenance and wear a smile. The Lord will reward your effort. Gradually, you may graduate from selling on the roadside to a shop, and be noted as a peanut specialist. Some day you may have opportunity to package peanuts for export. Then you will remember this little solution. So, arise from your poverty lifestyle and be somebody, in Jesus name. Amen!!

DECISION

If you sincerely want healing, and deliverance for your soul and spirit, then you need to rededicate your life to the Lord Jesus Christ. Confess your errors and faults. Make restitution where necessary. Repent before the Lord and lay your life on the altar of sacrifice. Then you will receive a touch of the Holy Spirit and your broken heart will be healed as the hurts and bitterness roll away. God bless you as you do this. Amen, and Amen.

SALVATION

If you have not given your life to Jesus Christ, this is a good opportunity for you to do so. Go on your knees and confess your sins. Then ask the Lord Jesus Christ to forgive you as you confess and repent that you ever lived as a sinner. Acknowledge the Lord Jesus Christ as the only One who can save and set you free from sin. Then ask the Lord Jesus Christ to come into your life and change your pattern of life. Tell Him to take control over you. Tell Him to help you to overcome the past and take you through the life that leads into the kingdom of God. Your life will never be the same again. God bless you. Amen!!

Poetic Expression Eight

ARISE FROM CAPTIVITY

Arise from captivity
And fear no foe
Rebuke the enemy
And he shall flee from you
Renounce his control over you
Release your character from deception
And you shall be an Overcomer.

Arise from captivity
And break the chains of fear
Reach out for your weapons
And mount up the offensive position
Raise your voice against iniquity
And reverse your situation
Then you shall be an Overcomer

Arise from captivity
And possess your possession
Proclaim His Word
And release your authority
Shout with joy
And praise His Holy name
Establish yourself as an Overcomer

Arise from captivity
And claim your victory
Sing aloud
And suppress the enemy

Dance around
And subdue the land
Establish yourself as an Overcomer

Pauline Walley, November 1996.

Chapter Eight

LEGAL GROUNDS

Isaiah 61:2,

...To proclaim the acceptable year of the Lord and the day of vengeance of our God.

L egal grounds are the original plans that God had for you from the beginning of creation. It is the possession that God gave you in the Garden of Eden. It is your richness, wealth and possession in Christ Jesus.

KNOW YOUR LEGAL GROUNDS

Before the creation of mankind, the Lord had already created all other things, and set the stage for man to enjoy the work of His hands.

Genesis 1:24-31 says,

Then God said, "Let the earth bring forth the living creatures according to its kind; cattle and creeping things and beasts of the earth, each according to its kind;" and

it was so. And God made the beasts of the earth according to its kind, cattle according to its kind, and everything that creeps on the earth according to its kind. And God saw that it was good. Then God said, "Let us make man in Our image, according to Our likeness; let them have dominion over the fish of the sea, over the birds of the air, and over the cattle, over all the earth and over every creeping thing that creeps on the earth." So God created man in His own image; in the image of God He created him; male and female He created them. Then God blessed them, and God said to them, "Be fruitful and multiply; fill the earth and subdue it; have dominion over the fish of the sea, over the birds of the air, and over every living thing that moves on the earth." And God said, "See, I have given you every herb that yields seed which is on the face of all the earth, and every tree whose fruit yields seed; to you it shall be for food...Then God saw everything that He had made, and indeed it was very good."

Now this passage reveals the in-depth of your legal grounds of existence above all other things that exist on earth. You must take a special note that you are created in the image of God. You must also note that everything that God made is very good and perfect. Since God is the only perfect One, then everything about your life must be in good shape or perfect standard. Therefore, you cannot attribute any evil or misfortune that befalls you to God the perfect Creator.

Why would God contradict His Word and inflict your body with ailment and frustrate your life, when He created you in His personal image to take care of this world? He is neither wicked nor aimless, neither does He fail nor disappoint. Why then do we have troubles and sicknesses? Why do some of His creatures suffer if it is not part of His plan and purpose?

THE ENTANGLEMENT

The cause of the imperfection in your life today is the sinful lifestyle that reflects in your character, behavior and attitude, which entangles and drives one into the camp of the enemy, where Satan holds one in bondage. The entangled life began with the disobedience of mankind (Adam and Eve) in the Garden of Eden as mentioned earlier on.

It is surprising that many people including churchgoers are not quite sure of the exact sin that caused the downfall of humankind. Some do refer to the original sin as "sex;" while others think it is the eating of the forbidden "apple." Now get it right. The sin committed was neither *sex nor the eating of an apple,* as commonly believed. The main sin was disobedience to God's command—thus eating from the tree of life.

The Command
Genesis 2:16-17,

And the Lord God commanded the man, saying, "Of every tree of the garden you may freely eat; <u>but of the tree of the knowledge of good and evil you shall not eat</u>, for in the day that you eat of it you shall surely die. [*Underlining by author.*]

The Disobedience
Genesis 3:6,

So when the woman saw that the tree was good for food, that it was pleasant to the eyes, and a tree desirable to make one wise, <u>she took of its fruit and ate</u>. She also gave to her husband with her, and he ate.
[*Underlining by author.*]

WHY THE DISOBEDIENCE?

The disobedience started when Eve gave attention to the serpent. She opened up freely to it, and they had quite a long conversation, during which time the enemy tried to convince her to disobey the Lord's command. Eve had the authority to rebuke the serpent. She also had the power to resist it and send it away from her. But she did not. She refused to utilize her power and authority. Instead, she submitted her dominion to the serpent, and wasted her authority when she welcomed the suggestion to perform the act of eating the fruit. She gave the idea a thought, and then decided to implement it. Since that day, she lost her power and authority that the Lord God gave mankind in Genesis 1:26 (above).

In practice, many people like to entertain negative suggestions, both in their mind, and with ungodly persons. An action is often the follow-up of a thought that had been nurtured for quite a while. One would have pondered and considered the effects. However, the final decision is supported by the controlling force, or the authority to which one easily submits—either to the Lordship of Jesus Christ or to the controlling forces of darkness.

One step leads to the other, until the plan matures. Learn to rebuke any thought or conversation that is ungodly and unscriptural. If you are not sure of what you hear, cross-check with the Scriptures. If you are confused, fast and pray and ask God to reveal the truth to you.

The satanic conversation
Genesis 3:1-5,

Now the serpent was more cunning than any beast of the field which the Lord God had made. And he said to the woman, "Has God indeed said, 'You shall not eat of every tree of the garden?'" And the woman said to the serpent, "We may eat the fruit of the trees of the garden; but of the fruit of the tree which is in the midst of the garden, God has said, 'You shall not eat it, nor shall you touch it, lest you die.'" And the serpent said to the woman, "You will not surely die. For God knows that in the day you eat of it your eyes will be opened, and you will be like God, knowing good and evil." [*Underlining by author.*]

Following this sin, man was cursed. The end result of the curses placed upon man is the various evils that befall mankind. However, shortly after the curses had been pronounced, the Lord also made provision for them to be reversed, so that the purpose of creation would be fulfilled.

THE CURSES

Both mankind and the serpent (the deceiver) were cursed for being co-participants in the act of the sin of disobedience. Although Eve lured Adam to it, both the husband and the wife suffered and were punished.

245

THE DECEIVER

The serpent that was acting on behalf of Satan the deceiver, the father of lies, was the first to receive its punishment.

Genesis 3:14-15 records,

And the Lord God said unto the serpent, "Because thou has done this, thou art cursed above all cattle, and above every beast of the field; upon thy belly shalt thou go, and dust shalt thou eat all the days of thy life: And I will put enmity between thee and the woman, and between thy seed and her seed; it shall bruise thy head, and thou shalt bruise his heel.

Following this curse, the serpent is the only specie of reptiles that has no legs, and so has to crawl on its belly. There has been no time when the serpent has been a friend to any human being. At a glimpse of each other's sight, each runs a different direction. On some occasions, there is often a great fight between the two. The serpent's target is often to bite the heel of the man, while man's target is to bruise the serpent's head. If the serpent is mistakenly cut by the tail or in the middle, it will fight back until its mouth grabs something to bite.

This explains why the Lord God advised Moses to pick up the rod that turned into a serpent by the tail, but not by the head, else it would see him (Moses) as an enemy. Under the discussion on *"Spiritual Captivity"* in Chapter Four, an instance was cited of a couple that kept a python snake as a pet. Of course the serpent could not hide its characteristics for too long. One morning the nine-foot long serpent launched an attack against the family, and held the woman bound in its mouth. The result of the curse is enmity.

THE WOMAN

The woman was the next to be punished. **Genesis 3:16 records,**

> **To the woman He said: "I will greatly multiply your sorrow and your conception; In pain you shall bring forth children; Your desire shall be for your husband, and he shall rule over you."**

"I WILL GREATLY MULTIPLY YOUR SORROW AND CONCEPTION"

This curse is strongly binding on women. Many go through difficult times in marriage. One of the major sorrows is barrenness; and another is conception pain.

Barrenness

The ability to fulfill the blessings of fruitfulness as commanded, "Be fruitful and multiply…" was hindered from the moment the curse was released. Many women go through a time of barrenness. Some wait a very long time before they are able to conceive; some do not have the opportunity to bear children, as they are never released. Others who are able to bear children are fruitful for a while, until they encounter menopause. Menopause is part of the curse, because the blessing did not place limitation on life span.

Conception Pain

The sorrow of conception causes women to go through various levels of body pain and sicknesses such as menstrual pain, and labor pain. There are cases when some women experience some sort of ailment throughout their menstruation period. Some women do not menstruate at all, and require medical assistance. Many women suffer different various ailments during the nine-month period of pregnancy. Some survive labor pain and some die. All the difficult situations that women encounter during menstruation, pregnancy and birthing are the effects of the curse that was placed on the woman in the Garden of Eden (Genesis 3).

REVERSE THE CURSE

If you have a close relationship with God, you can reverse this curse upon your life. Remind God of His promises, hold firm to the Scripture, make it your point of reference, and reclaim your promises stating that you are no longer in the camp of Satan since Jesus came into your life. Proclaim that you have been redeemed by the blood of the Lamb. Proclaim that you have returned to the Garden of Eden (the kingdom of God) and you are no longer under the control of Satan. Walk out of your captivity and step into the liberty of the Lord Jesus Christ. Make these your points of reference:

Sarah

God reversed the curse of menopause on behalf of Sarah, Abraham's wife, for the sake of the promised child Isaac. Amazingly, Sarah conceived and delivered the child Isaac at an old age, while Abraham was one hundred years old.

Hannah

Hannah, a barren woman, touched the heart of God with a vow, and gave birth to Samuel who became the last Judge in Israel. Samuel was the prophet who anointed the first king of Israel, Saul, and the second king, David.

Manoah

Manoah and his wife had given up, when God decided to show them mercy, and Samson was born.

Zachariah and Elizabeth

Zachariah and Elizabeth had resigned their fate, having passed the age of child bearing. Elizabeth had already experienced menopause when God decided to pour out a blessing unto her home and John the Baptist was conceived and delivered.

TESTIMONY OF BREAKING THE CURSE OF MENOPAUSE

I have come across some women who prayed and conceived at the time that medical personnel has declared that it was impossible for them to carry pregnancies or deliver babies. One of these women is Vickey.

Vickey was a prominent woman from Nigeria in West Africa. She gave her life to the Lord Jesus Christ shortly after she lost a son who was a dedicated Christian. Vickey called upon the Lord to give her another son, since she had passed the age of childbearing. She was then in her 40s.

In her petition, Vickey also reminded the Lord that the curse of labor pain in pregnancy and delivery was meant for the ungodly woman, so now that she was a new creation in Christ Jesus, that curse of sorrow should no longer apply to her. Also, Vickey asked the Lord to grant her knowledge of the time and season when the child would be delivered.

The Lord granted Vickey all that she had requested. Vickey's delivery experience passed on like a film show, as doctors and midwives could not understand the short and easy delivery that took place within a twinkle of an eye. The doctors had taught that she was out of her senses when she notified them of her own date and time of delivery. They did not take her seriously when she arrived the hospital to deliver her baby boy. Neither did they believe when she told them the exact time to receive the baby.

The Lord God had set His ministering hosts around Vickey to assist her. Vickey, in her confidence in the work of the Holy Spirit, held on to the promise of God. Today she is a testimony unto many who have learned to reverse the curse that causes labor pain. Glory be to God.

During my teenage days I went through serious menstrual pains. I suffered terrible headache and body pain during my menstrual period. At a point I suffered irregularities, and was put on medication. This cost my parents a fortune, as I was put under regular care of a private doctor.

At a point, the doctors could not understand the trauma that I was going through. According to them, the complications were not normal with menstruation, so they were thinking of surgery. This meant another set of medications, and an increase in medical bills for my parents. The more I listened to the doctors discuss my issue, the more my thoughts were focused on the Lord Jesus as the only Physician I could depend on. The strenuous part of it all was that every month, I had to travel many miles from school for my checkup.

During one of these visits, I was given a wrong medication. By God's grace, I detected the strange tablets when I got home, and immediately returned to complain to the doctor. He looked at me and said, "You would have to pay another one hundred pounds to get a new set of tablets."

I tried to explain to him that it was not my fault but he insisted that I pay the bill. I returned home that afternoon, not with the intention of getting the money from my parents, but with the decision to seek the Great Physician. On the way home, that afternoon of 1977, I wept and cried to the Lord Jesus Christ to deliver me from whatever ailment that had captured my life.

Within that period, my "Bible knowledge" class was studying the book of Samuel, in which I had learned about Hannah. All of a sudden the story of Hannah and the birth of Samuel dawned on me. I spent the rest of the day reading through that passage. I held to it as my point of reference to claim my healing. Indeed, the Lord heard my prayer and granted my request. Since 1977 till this date, I have had no cause to seek medical assistance over that issue. Praise the Lord.

IN PAIN YOU SHALL BRING FORTH CHILDREN

To many women, rearing children is just as painful as delivery pain in the "labor room." Although the experience of having the children is a great joy to all mothers, each of them has a tale of woe to recount.

Sometimes the various stages of a child's development attract ailments and so much attention from the parents. The teething and the toddling stage, as well as the feeding of babies, could be traumatic for some parents.

Similarly, the teenage and youthful exuberance demand parental attention. Attention deficiency syndrome can sometimes lead to juvenile delinquency and uncontrolled behavioral attitude if not checked out early enough to avoid it.

Many mothers pray day and night, hoping for the survival of their young ones. They do not eat until the children have eaten. Neither do they sleep until the children have slept. They sacrifice their bodies for pain and endure all sorts of agony for the sake of their children. It is even worse if their fathers are irresponsible or do not understand the essence of fatherly devotion.

REVERSE THE CURSE

Reverse the curse of a trend of behavior and attitude that exists in your family—on your mother's side and your father's side. Pray against any common traits that you are aware of. Break the link and continuation from your children (the born and unborn ones alike). Plead the blood of Jesus Christ to cover their character and behavior.

Set your family free from the negative things that ever existed in your own lives as parents. Ensure that your children do not inherit any negative or ungodly character that you once displayed in your lives, including that of your childhood and teenage years. Whatever is not good biblically is never good, no matter what you feel about it. Face the reality and reject them. Check the chapter on *Physical Captivity* for the character traits you have noticed.

YOUR DESIRE SHALL BE FOR YOUR HUSBAND

Indeed women always look up to men for marriage. No matter how much a woman may admire and like a man, unless the man has a similar desire and expresses it, the woman's desire remains with her. More so, some women suffer a lot of neglect and rejection from men. This has contributed to broken homes/marriages.

AND HE SHALL RULE OVER YOU

No matter how intelligent or beautiful a woman may be, her husband is forever the head in the home. The Scripture says the husband is the head of the family, even as Christ is the head of the Church. This is the only part of the curse that cannot be changed, because Jesus Christ sanctioned and established it. However, this particular authority has been greatly utilized by some ungodly men who treat their wives like slaves.

To this category of men, women have no say in the home. Women are seen as the evil that causes the downfall of men. And so their suggestions are nothing less than evil. This type of men operates their homes like a factory, where no friendly conversation is ever held. The only time such husbands interact freely with their wives is when there are guests around. Other than that, all other utterances are restricted to "demand" and "supply."

This curse also influences the decision of men in marriage. In some cultural settings men have the authority to marry as many wives as they can afford, and also employ the services of concubines in addition. But a woman dares not be found courting more than one man at a time. She would be stoned to death.

Sometimes divorced women are treated like outcasts in certain parts of the world because of the curse. No man would want to remarry a divorcee, because they had once exposed their bodies to men, and are regarded as just prostitutes for that same reason. Unfortunately, the men involved easily pick up new partners without fears, yet they are always welcomed.

REVERSE THE CURSE

Woman, hold on to the fact that the Lord God has said that a man shall leave his father and mother to be joined with a woman. And the two of them shall be one flesh. Therefore, that man (your husband) is one flesh with you. The man is your bone and the woman his flesh.

Pray unity into your home. Pray his soul back home. Cause his own desire to be unto you as yours is unto him.

Call his attention to the fact that his desire is meant for you alone, and not unto another, because God said two shall be one, not three or four.

Pray all the blessings of marriage into your home as the Scripture says. If he is living in any form of captivity, then it is your duty to pray and seek for his deliverance. Ask the Lord for direction so that he will walk out of it and into a place where he will meet the Lord. You cannot throw your husband away, just as you wouldn't reject your own son. Husbands are like babies unto the women to whom they are married. Ask God for wisdom to deal with his weaknesses and nurture your husband.

THE MAN

Although the man was not part of the initial plot to disobey the command of the Lord, he suffered part of the punishment. This is because he did not warn his wife against entertaining the deceiver. He also failed to correct her, when she was going astray. Rather, he compromised; which means that he was a co-participant in the sin. For that reason, he was cursed with poverty. He lost all the good riches and wealth with which he had been blessed. The gold and the silver were taken out of his reach. He now had to struggle for his daily bread.

Genesis 3:17-19 says,

Then to Adam he said, "Because you have heeded the voice of your wife, and have eaten from the tree of which I commanded you, saying, `You shall not eat of it'; Cursed is the ground for your sake; In toil you shall eat of it all the days of your life. Both thorns and thistles it shall bring forth for you, and you shall eat the herb of the field. In the sweat of your face you shall eat bread till you return to the ground, for out of it you were taken; For dust you are, and to dust you shall return."

ANALYSIS FROM GRACE TO GRASS

The Curse of Poverty

When a rich man is stripped off his wealth, and all that he once had, he will be left with nothing. He will be referred as "used to." He is now a poor man. This was the case of the first man, Adam.

Initially, Adam was a prosperous man. He was surrounded with diverse wealth both in the spiritual realm and in the physical. He was blessed with silver and gold as well as material possessions. He had more than he ever bargained for. Adam was also a man of authority, and had dominion over everything on earth. He was fruitful and had great potential for multiplication in all facets of his life (**Genesis 1:28-30**).

Adam lost every bit of the great wealth the day he disobeyed the Lord's command. His authority was taken from him and he was made poor instantly. He was driven out of his original home—the Garden of Eden. He left the

Garden empty handed—poor in spirit and poor in wealth. He also lost the presence of God, and became a dead man living in the flesh. This is how poverty came about. So it is obvious that <u>poverty is a curse</u> that came as a result to <u>disobedience to the command of God</u>. **"...for in the day that you eat of it you shall surely die" (Genesis 2:17).**

REVERSE THE CURSE OF POVERTY

Shortly after the sin was committed, the Lord God promised to send the Savior to redeem man from the curse. Therefore, when mankind corrupted the earth, the Lord erased both the sinners and the whole earth with a flood, but saved the life of the righteous man—Noah, and his household.

While preparing the lineage of the Savior, another corruption going on in the land of Sodom and Gomorrah caught the attention of God. Hence, that city was consumed by fire along with the dwellers, yet, the life of another righteous man—Lot and his household—was saved, except for his disobedient wife who turned into the pillar of salt.

During the various stages as the coming of the Savior was being prepared, several evils were committed that did not go without punishment. Those who repented and showed remorse were pardoned and forgiven. Such persons' lives were also saved from damnation.

King David was one of the people who exploited the grace of God proficiently. He was quick to repent, and easily admitted his sin and submitted to corrections. The three major men (Abraham, Jacob/Israel and David) that carried the covenant and strength of the Savior committed offenses at one time or the other in their lives. Because they repented, God pardoned them.

These three personalities enjoyed great wealth and God's prosperity and health as well as long life. Although

God had cursed the earth, yet He promised and blessed them abundantly. This is to say that God did not originally intend for man to be poor. Poverty was not part of His original plan and purpose. It is His perfect and gracious will that mankind will prosper and be in good health. As Apostle John expresses it in

3 John 3:2 (KJV),

Beloved, I wish above all things that thou mayest prosper and be in health, even as thy soul prospereth.

He is the same God who promised to bless the children of Israel with the land that flows with milk and honey. Abraham is the father of faith. Every righteous person who confesses Jesus Christ as Lord and Savior is an heir to the throne. Therefore, such persons are princes and princesses in the kingdom of God. The children of the kingdom have access to the riches and prosperity that exist within the palace. That is why the Lord Jesus Christ said that **no child asks for bread to be given a stone; neither does anyone who asks for fish receive a serpent**.

As a result of the promises you are entitled to the riches of the Kingdom.

- Claim your portion of the promise and possess your possession.
- Reject the curse, and hold on to the promise.
- Speak the promises into your life by quoting the appropriate Scriptures.
- Declare your stand in Christ Jesus as a redeemed child bought with a price and washed in the blood of the Lamb.

- Shout it over the mountaintop that Jesus Christ is Lord of your life; old things are passed away and new things have come.

The new things that were promised include your riches and prosperity in the spirit, in the physical, in the material blessings and in finance.

- Start to pray by calling your name...(Pauline) and say to your soul, body and spirit, "There is no more lack. I receive my riches and prosperity."
- Make a list of the things you lack, and begin to call them into reality as you renounce the curse of poverty.
- Claim your freedom from the chains and grip of Satan.
- Set your soul and spirit free from all entanglements.

DISENTANGLE YOUR LIFE FROM CAPTIVITY

In order to disentangle your life from any form of captivity, you need to make conscious effort to walk out of it. Separate yourself from the things that entangle you.

SEPARATION

When you visit the doctor for medical treatment, you consciously obey every possible treatment he recommends. You consciously observe the rules and possibly live by them all the days of your life. Some rules like avoiding sugar (diabetics), meat, milk, egg, etc have been kept as strict rules in people's diet just to ensure healing in line with medical rules.

If a medical rule, made by a scientist (human being) can be so binding on people, then a greater place must be given to the Creator of mankind. There is no other Physician like the Lord Jesus Christ. Believe His word, and separate yourself from the things that entangle you.

SEPARATION FROM CORRUPTION

Corruption was the cause of Noah's flood that marked the destruction of the whole earth. Therefore resist corruption. Do not be afraid to maintain your righteousness. Determine to be the first devoted righteous person in your community and family.

Genesis 6:11-13 says,

So God looked upon the earth, and indeed it was corrupt; for all flesh had corrupted their way on the earth. And God said to Noah, "The end of all flesh has come before Me, for the earth is filled with violence through them; and behold, I will destroy them with the earth.

SEPARATION UNTO SALVATION

In order to receive and maintain your deliverance, sometimes you might need to separate from the members of your family and relatives who are involved in satanic worship or from the people in your environment who are involved in occult.

Genesis 12:1-2 says,

Now the Lord had said to Abram: "Get out of your country, From your kindred, and from your father's house, to a land that I will show you. I will make you a great nation; and I will bless you..."

Abraham did not get blessed until he had separated completely from his relatives, Tarah his father and Lot his nephew.

SEPARATION FROM SEXUAL SIN

We need to be conscious of the fact that sexual sin (*Physical Captivity*) was one of the major reasons why the cities of Sodom and Gomorrah were destroyed during the time of Abraham. The Lord had cultivated friendship with Abraham in order that he would command his children and his household after him; that they keep the way of the Lord, to do righteousness and justice; that the promise of the birth of the Savior might be fulfilled through him (Abraham) as the Lord had spoken.

In view of the promise, when an outcry came up against Sodom and Gomorrah because they were involved in sexual sin (homosexuality and lesbianism), which was described as grievous, the Lord decided to go down and see whether they had done altogether according to the outcry against it. The sins of the people were so grievous that they even attempted to attack the Lord's messengers for sexual harassment— homosexuality—until they were struck with blindness.

Genesis 19:5, 15-17 says,

And they called to Lot and said to him, "Where are the men who came to you tonight? <u>Bring them out to us that we may know them carnally</u> [*sexually assault, homosexuality*]. When the morning dawned, the angels urged Lot to hurry, saying, "<u>Arise, take your wife and your two daughters who are here, lest you be consumed in the punishment of the city</u>." And while he lingered, the men took hold of his hand, his wife's hand, and the hands of his two daughters, the Lord being merciful to him, and they brought him out and set him outside the city...<u>Escape for your life</u>! Do not look behind you nor stay anywhere in the plain. <u>Escape to the mountains, lest you be destroyed</u>. [*Underlining by author.*]

SEPARATION FROM MATERIAL CAPTIVITY

Achan the troubler of Israel: One man's greediness for material wealth could affect a whole nation. The lust for material wealth can have a negative impact on a nation.

Joshua 7:1, 20, 21, 25 records,

But the children of Israel committed a trespass regarding the accursed things, for Achan the son of Carmi, ...took of the accursed things; so the anger of the Lord burned against the children of Israel...

And Achan answered Joshua and said, "Indeed I have sinned against the Lord God of Israel, and this is what I have done:

"When I saw among the spoils <u>a beautiful Babylonian garment, two hundred shekels of silver, and a wedge of gold weighing fifty shekels, I coveted them and took them</u>. And there they are, hidden in the earth in the midst of my tent, with the silver under it..."

And Joshua said, "Why have you troubled us? The Lord will trouble you this day." So all Israel stoned him with stones; and they burned them with fire after they had stoned them with stones." [*Underlining by author.*]

SEPARATION FROM REBELLION

A rebel is anyone who kicks against the authority of leadership, especially against ministers of God. It also refers to people who raise false accusations against ministers, or those who are prone to faultfinding against ministrations and other ministerial duties—preaching, teaching, or praying. If you spot an error in a minister, pray and fast that the Lord will convict him/her unto repentance.

Ministers are humans who are privileged to be God's servants; therefore God is their Master (the big Boss). Just report any fault to their Master on your knees and He will deal with them accordingly. Do not pose to be the perfect man, seeking a perfect fellowship/church.

Do not imply that since you have a high taste for righteousness, your wish should prevail over others' authority.

Be careful. Otherwise, Satan will use you to kick against the authority of God.

Satan himself is a rebel, and the father of rebels. He (Satan) kicked against the authority of God; that is why he is the enemy of the gospel of our Lord Jesus Christ. He was the one who convinced Adam and Eve to kick against the command of God in the Garden of Eden, so beware of his devices.

King David refused to lift his finger against King Saul who made several attempts to kill him. David recognized the fact that Saul was appointed and anointed by God. He had the opportunity for revenge, but he knew God would not be happy with him. If you <u>speak against the minister of God or you accuse him, be it true or false, you will lose your peace and will live in torment until you confess and repent</u>. That was why King David, after one of his encounters with Saul in **1 Chronicles 16:22** and **Psalm 105:15, declared, "<u>Do not touch my anointed ones, and do my prophets no harm</u>."** [*Underlining by author.*]

Although King Saul was senior to David in the ministry of leadership, King Saul lost his peace and lived under torment as long as he hated and envied "Little David" for his brilliant talents and performances. Miriam and Aaron were of the same parentage as Moses. The two siblings (Miriam and Aaron) worked together to support Moses leadership. Yet, when they criticized Moses over an issue of marriage, God did not spare them. This is because an attempt to lift a finger against Moses the leader meant opposing the authority of God. The act of rebellion could encourage others to disobey or reject Moses' authority.

Number 12:1-14,

Then Miriam and Aaron SPOKE AGAINST MOSES because of the

Ethiopian woman whom he had married; …And they said, "<u>Has the Lord indeed spoken only through Moses? Has he not spoken through us also</u>?" And the Lord heard it. (Now the man Moses was very humble, more than all men who were on the face of the earth.) Suddenly the Lord said to Moses, Aaron, and Miriam, "Come out, you three, to the tabernacle of meeting! …Then the Lord came down in the pillar of cloud and stood in the door of the tabernacle, and called Aaron and Miriam. And both went forward. Then He said, "Hear now My words: If there is a prophet among you, I, the Lord, make Myself known to him in a vision, And I speak to him in a dream. Not so with My servant Moses; He is faithful in all My house. <u>I speak to him face to face, even plainly, and not in dark sayings</u>; and he sees the form of the Lord. Why then were you not afraid to speak against My servant Moses?" So the anger of the Lord was aroused against them, and He departed. And then the cloud departed from above the tabernacle; <u>suddenly Miriam became leprous</u>, as white as snow. Then Aaron turned toward Miriam, and there she was a leper. So Aaron said to Moses, "Oh, my Lord! Please do not lay this sin on us, in which we have done foolishly and in which we have sinned. Please do not let her be as one dead, whose flesh is half consumed when he comes out of his mother's womb!" So Moses cried out to he

Lord, saying, "Please heal her, O God, I pray!" Then the Lord said to Moses, "If her father had but spit in her face, would she not be shamed seven days? Let her be shut out of the camp seven days, and after that she may be received again." So Miriam was shut out of the camp seven days, and the people did not journey on till Miriam was brought in again. [*Underlining by author.*]

Beloved, you will notice that God came down to defend Moses. That is why we need to be very careful of what we say about the ministers of God. A minister is said to be the "apple of God's eye." We should not expect them to operate the way we think or feel. Remember that "God's ways are not our ways, neither are His thoughts our thoughts." Leave them alone for God to judge and punish.

If you are a sincere child of God, always make time out periodically to pray and fast for your pastors and other notable ministers (personally known and unknown to you). Your intercession will yield positive results and God will reward you for taking care of His prophets. For instance way back in 1979, after reading about a woman of God— *Kathryn Kulhman: Daughter of Destiny*—I had a burden to begin an intercessory prayer for ministers of God.

The Lord increased my spiritual gifts because of that, as He will always reveal the area of their needs to me. I don't have any personal relationships with Billy Graham, Kenneth Hagin, Benson Idahosa or Benny Hinn; yet I prayed for them consistently up to this date. Any time I hear a negative comment about a minister of God, I know it is time to pray and intercede for such a person. You will not gain anything talking about other people's faults or finding fault with them; but you will be blessed abundantly if you pray for ministers.

In 1993, the Lord gave me a burden to pray for one of the renowned evangelists (Billy Graham) in the United States against an ailment of his body. Within that week I met a Baptist pastor in Wales (U.K) who was trying to find out my area of ministration. Then I told him about my intercessory ministry, which enables me to have knowledge about people and the area of their needs; so I cited the current burden I had for the healing of the American Evangelist Billy Graham. Immediately, the Baptist pastor interrupted and asked, "How do you know, this is very true. His personal assistant just mentioned that to me yesterday. I don't think anyone knows about it because it has just happened..." Then he said, "Please, can you preach in my church on Sunday?" Ministering in his assembly opened doors for intercession for the salvation of souls in Wales and other parts of Britain.

Imagine what would have happened if I had indulged in criticizing or finding fault with other ministers; would I have had the opening for ministration? I might even have lost my own anointing as other people also set their hearts on finding faults and raising false accusations against me and the ministry that the Lord has committed to me.

This is not to say that you necessarily face such trials because you were once involved. I face a lot of false accusations, and the Lord has always defended me in His own way. I just need to be watchful and ensure that I don't offend fellow ministers deliberately. Anytime the Holy Spirit convicts me on such accounts, I go out to apologize, so that I don't face the wrath of God.

Once I was trying to lay hands on a sister during prayer, I felt a force push me back, away from her; then I heard a voice say, "How dare you touch her, when you have ought against her." Immediately, I knew that was the voice of the God of Holiness. So I stopped the prayer and confessed and apologized to her. She also apologized for the offense and we asked God for cleansing by the blood of Jesus Christ; after which we thanked God for the correction and continued the prayer. Not too long afterward I began to prophesy in her mother's tongue (Ebo Language), which I didn't understand nor have ever spoken in my life.

Since she understood the language, she received the interpretation. It was a personal issue for which she was seeking God's face, yet it took my repentant heart to move the hands of God. Please do not lay hands (during prayer) on anybody you are not in agreement with. It is dangerous. Even if you are a minister (pastor, teacher, evangelist, prophet or apostle) no matter how talented or highly respected you are, do not speak against another minister in public. Pray for your offenders, and call the person's attention to the errors committed.

Any time a minister criticizes another in the open, the work of God suffers, because it gives an opening for the enemy to attack other ministers. At that point, one will be ridiculing the Word of God to the advantage of workers of iniquity. It also means that the body of Christ is divided. And the Lord warned us against division of the body of Christ. Like the High Priest, the minister involved will be "re-nailing" Jesus Christ to the cross.

Korah and other leaders rebelled against Moses and Aaron. They criticized Moses and Aaron's spirituality and expressed jealousy for their anointing,

Numbers 16:1-31,

They gathered together against Moses and Aaron, and said to them. You take too much upon yourselves, for the entire congregation is holy, every one of them, and the Lord is among them. Why then do you exalt yourselves above the congregation of the Lord?

So when Moses heard it he fell on His face...the ground split apart under them, and the earth opened its mouth and swallowed them up, with their households and all the men with Korah, with all their goods. So they and all those with them went down alive into the pit; the earth closed over them, and they perished from among the congregation...

Note that you will not go "unpunished" if you criticize or rebel or accuse an anointed man/woman of God.

SEPARATION FROM SELFISH AMBITION, DISOBEDIENCE, AND PRIDE

It is pertinent to note that public position in the corridor of powers; prosperity in riches, wealth and treasures; title, fame or any other achievements are no licenses for disobedience, pride and selfishness; especially in a situation where instructions or directives are given with regard to the work of God at any point in time.

1 Samuel 15:1-23 says,

Samuel also said to Saul, "The Lord sent me to anoint you king over His people, over Israel. Now therefore, heed the voice of the words of the Lord. Thus says the Lord of hosts: 'I will punish Amalek for what he did to Israel, how he laid wait for him on the way when he came up from Egypt. Now go and attack Amalek, and utterly destroy all that they have, and do not spare them. But kill both man and

woman, infant and nursing child, ox and sheep, camel and donkey.'"...but Saul and the people spared Agag **and the best of the sheep, the oxen, the fatlings, the lambs, and all that was good, and were unwilling to utterly destroy them. But everything disposed and worthless, that they utterly destroyed. Now the word of the Lord came to Samuel, saying, "I greatly regret that I have set up Saul as king, for he has turned his back from following Me, and has not performed my Commandments." And it grieved Samuel, and he cried out to the Lord all night...** Saul went to Carmel, and indeed, **he set up a monument for himself...** Then Samuel said, **"Has the Lord any great delight in burnt offerings and sacrifices? As in obeying the voice of the Lord? Behold, to obey is better than sacrifice, and to heed than the fat of rams. For rebellion is as the sin of witchcraft, and stubbornness is as iniquity and idolatry. Because you have rejected the word of God, He also has rejected you from being king." "...The Lord has torn the kingdom of Israel from you today, and has given it to a neighbor of yours, who is better than you." ...And Samuel went no more to see Saul until the day of his death.** [*Underlining by author.*]

Disobedience to authority is a sin. Many people want to serve God and do the things of God only when it is convenient and feel like doing it. Because it is "voluntary," they should be allowed to do it on their own volition. Otherwise, they feel pressurized and embarrassed.

More so, some people think that if God wants them to participate in certain activities...then God must talk to them, because they can equally hear God as the minister does. So until God speaks to them, the minister has no right to instruct them. In fact, such individuals think that coming to church is meant to help the pastor raise funds (tithes and offerings) for the ministry. To such individuals, going to church means sympathizing with the minister in charge.

Beloved, if this is your thought and idea, then it is time to REPENT, for the kingdom of God is at hand, and Satan could be knocking at your doorstep. Once again, be careful not to walk in disobedience.

Deuteronomy 23:9-14 says,

When the army goes out against your enemies, then keep yourself from every wicked thing. If there is any man among you who becomes unclean by some occurrence in the night, then he shall go outside the camp; he shall not come inside the camp. But it shall be, when evening comes, that he shall wash himself with water; and when the sun sets, he may come into the camp again. Also you shall have a place outside the camp, where you may go out; and you shall have an implement among your equipment, and when you sit down outside, you shall dig with it and turn and cover your refuse. For the Lord your God walks in the midst of your camp, to deliver you and give your enemy over to you, and turn away from you.
[*Underlining by author.*]

THE PROCESS OF DELIVERANCE

In order to achieve effective liberty in deliverance, the affected victim must give consent; otherwise, it will be difficult to get release. This is because the controlling demons know when you desire to abhor them. Your behavior and attitude toward deliverance ministration either influences their presence or drives them away. These are some of the major points you need to observe in order to receive effective deliverance ministration:

ADMITTANCE

The victim must <u>admit</u> the fact that he/she is in a type of captivity or bondage; and that the situation is a sign of satanic or demonic oppression, controlled by powers and principalities of darkness.

> **Matthew 15:22,**
>
> **And behold, a woman of Canaan came from that region and cried out to Him, saying, "Have mercy on me, O Lord, Son of David! <u>My daughter is severely demon possessed</u>.** [*Underlining by author.*]

This woman recognized the fact that her daughter was being held in captivity, and she admitted it. Therefore she made an effort to seek deliverance.

WILLINGNESS

The victim <u>must be willing</u> to be delivered from his/her situation, having admitted that the problem is a sort of demonic captivity.

Matthew 15:23,

But He answered her not a word. And His disciples came and urged Him, saying, "Send her away, for <u>she cries after us</u>."

The woman <u>persisted</u> for deliverance, showing her <u>willingness</u> to break every demonic covenant and association with Satan.

SURRENDER

The victim must be <u>willing to surrender</u> himself/herself totally. The victim must also be willing to surrender all demonic items that are in his/her possession. Other than that, the minister will be wasting time and energy in an attempt to cast out the demons.

Sometimes some of the victims are in a lifetime covenant, which they are not quite ready to renounce or surrender because of the fear of losing an existing protection.

Matthew 15:24-25,

"...I was not sent except to the lost sheep of the house of Israel." Then she came and worshipped Him, saying, "Lord, help me!" The woman convinced the Lord that she was no longer going to worship any other god, but the Lord God Almighty through the Lord and Savior Jesus Christ.

To register her intention, she knelt down and lifted up her hands in total surrender to the Lordship of Jesus Christ. She renounced Satan and made an open decision.

CONFESSION

The victim must be willing to confess his/her involvement in any act that pertains to taking an oath with one's blood, soul, spirit or body in some form of occultic involvement. Oaths taken in form of covenant, vows, pledges or promises made in secrecy must be confessed so that one can receive total release during ministration.

Matthew 15:26-27,

But He answered and said, "It is not good to take the children's bread and throw it to the little dogs. And she said, "True, Lord, yet even the little dogs eat the crumbs which fall from their masters' table."

This woman agreed to the fact that she was not qualified for deliverance because of her in-depth involvement in demonic activities and wickedness. Instead of taking offense from Jesus' statement, she persisted for deliverance. For instance, once I told a lady to go take off the "extension piece" attached to her hair braids, having discerned that the source was contaminated. This woman became offended and went to report me to her pastor. Her pastor did not find out the reason, but began to harbor bitterness against me. The Lord revealed the state of the pastor to me, and I approached him. Up to this date, the pastor has refused to accept the fact that that lady in his church has a controlling spirit.

Sometimes, while leading the worship service, the demon (controlling spirit) will throw the lady on the floor; then her chest and head will begin to move up and down. Yet the pastor thinks it is the "Holy Spirit" in action. Asking that lady to take off an artificial piece of hair that the devil used as an advantage to enter her soul is an example of the statement, "It is not good to take the children's bread and throw it to the little dogs" that Jesus made to the Canaanite woman, who recognized her own captivity.

RESTORATION

Restoration comes as soon as confession is made.

Matthew 15:28,

Then Jesus answered and said to her, "O woman, great is your faith! Let it be to you as you desire." And her daughter was healed from that very hour.

This woman surrendered her desires for Jesus. She relinquished every property of Satan in her possession. She gave away all the things that pertained to spiritual, material, physical and emotional captivity, and claimed her deliverance desperately.

The conscious efforts she made to convince the Lord that she was willing and ready contributed to her restoration. You can apply this sample prayer to your situation and release your soul from captivity.

If you are not confident, seek the assistance of a mature Christian or minister of God to assist you. This prayer is to teach you to walk out of any captivity surrounding your life. You can make it. You can't be running around town every now and then searching for people to lay hands on you for petty things. Trust God for everything. Learn to utilize your authority. Amen. (See my book, *The Authority of an Overcomer* for details.)

THE PRAYER OF DELIVERANCE

Deliverance from the captivities discussed

My Lord and Savior Jesus Christ
I come to you just as I am
To ask for forgiveness of my sins
For the cleansing and purification of my soul
By the blood that you shed for me on the cross
I realize that the enemy has interfered
With my soul, body and spirit
I no longer want to compromise
Or participate in any action that is ungodly
Therefore I renounce every association
That I have ever had with Satan
I also renounce any form of covenant
I ever made with Satan knowingly and unknowingly.

Please mention any/all the covenants you are aware of and renounce all such in this manner…

I renounce every occultic and demonic covenant
That I made with the Metaphysics, Freemason, the Lodge,
Halloween, Obeah, Astrology, New Age spiritualism, etc …

I renounce your evil presence out of my life
in the name of Jesus
With the authority in the blood of Jesus
You shall no longer direct me or lead me
You shall no longer control me or my life
You shall no longer guide or protect me

Command them to stop performing any of the activities you are aware of… The blood of Jesus sets my spirit free
from your holds

I am free in the name of Jesus Christ...
I no longer belong to your demonic kingdom
In Jesus name, Amen!!

POSSESS YOUR POSSESSIONS

Now that you know the basics of your authority and possession in Christ Jesus, it will be wise for you to examine your gifts and talents.

- Pray and ask the Lord to teach you to utilize them for the glory of God in the fellowship in which you belong, and also to fetch you some ends-meet for your daily bread.

- Learn to utilize your talents out of nothing. Do not look up to people to assist you in any way before you take off, otherwise you will be disappointed and nothing may ever materialize. Just believe and trust God that your work will attract some attention and meet the Lord's favor. The Lord who has given you the talent will bless it and make it fruitful if you depend on Him. Amen...

By the grace of God, I published my first four albums and three books by faith at a time when I could not afford a meal. I trusted God for everything. The works were not perfect, yet they were "unique" in their own way, and met the needs of the people whom the Lord sent on my way. I have learned to trust God more than ever since the publication of my products, made simply out of talents without any form of support. Praise God from whom all blessings flow. Amen.

THE SIGNPOSTS TO HELL

- Note that only <u>one sin</u> committed caused the fall of mankind.

- Note that one first committed the offense, and the other one compromised, yet the two were punished.

- Note that only two persons were present at the scene of the offense, yet their children, great grand children and all the generations that follow to date, inherited the sin and its punishment (the curse).

Therefore, be warned that just one sin is enough to qualify anybody to be a candidate for hell (condemnation). All sins are equal and attract the same level of punishment (hell) before God. The only solution is confession and repentance and refrain from or resistance to sin. Share your testimony when it matures and make a public show of the enemy's deception.

Poetic Expression Nine

THOU SHALT NOT FORGET

I shall not forget
To maintain my deliverance
I shall remember
To resist temptation
I shall remember
To flee youthful lusts
I shall remember
To rebuke the enemy
I shall maintain my deliverance.

I shall not forget
To maintain my deliverance
I shall study
The Scriptures diligently
I shall study
And apply such to my life
I shall study
And demonstrate the reality
I shall maintain my deliverance.

I shall not forget
To maintain my deliverance
I shall learn
To counsel myself
I shall learn
To subdue negative thoughts
I shall learn
To examine my decisions
I shall maintain my deliverance.

I shall not forget
To maintain my deliverance
I shall make conscious effort
To educate myself
I shall make conscious effort
To examine my imaginations
I shall make conscious effort
To watch my character
I shall maintain my deliverance.

Pauline Walley, December 1996

Chapter Nine

MAINTAIN YOUR DELIVERANCE

Isaiah 61:2-3,

...To comfort all who mourn, To console whose who mourn in Zion...

Maintenance is one of the greatest solutions that mankind needs to manage life. No matter the level of success achieved in life, the ability to maintain it determines on how lasting the success will be. Many have attained great achievement within a short space of time, and have also lost it in the same manner. Some have also succeeded after a very long time of toiling and wailing, but lost everything because of lack of maintenance. Therefore, no matter what a person strives to achieve in this world, during the process of attainment, it is necessary to learn and adopt a maintenance culture.

Many people cry to the Lord for deliverance and healing everywhere, in all parts of the world. Although God answers by releasing revival into nations, churches and individual lives, little is done to maintain divine visitation. Surprisingly, some of the people and nations only have historical evidence, but not the reality of continuity because of lack of maintenance.

Today, many people wonder why their prayers are not answered. They think God is no longer in the business of answering prayers and releasing revival fire. Beloved, it is the Lord's desire to continue the outpouring of His Spirit upon us continuously. The problem is just with us, human beings. We often expect God to be stereotyped. To do things the same way as we think, or have seen it happen before. But His ways are not our ways, neither are His thoughts like ours. Unless we learn to be flexible, we will be in the continuous habit of losing whatever He gives to us. Maintenance is simply constant care, support, sustenance, preservation and proper management.

CONSCIOUS EFFORTS

In order for you to maintain your deliverance, you must determine to abstain totally from whatever has been the root cause of the former problems. Therefore:

- Make conscious efforts to put into practice your daily Scripture reading and studies.
- Make conscious efforts to live a righteous life (not religious or doctrinal rules) but a Bible believing and Holy Spirit-filled life.
- Make a conscious effort to speak the Word of God loud to yourself as though you are teaching or talking to someone. By this method, you will hear yourself speak positively and it will sink into your spirit and soul, therefore you shall not forget the precepts of God.
- Make a conscious effort to prepare your soul toward the coming of the Lord.

- Make a conscious effort to be sensitive to the Holy Spirit.
- Make a conscious effort to fast and pray for people around you. This is because if you do not help them spiritually to change their lives theirs may affect you.
- Make a conscious effort to avoid compromise with the world around you.
- Make a conscious effort to hold onto your deliverance as you would to a valuable asset or treasure.

PRAYER

I shall make a conscious effort to obey the Holy Spirit.

I shall make a conscious effort to...*(speak out positive words applicable to you)*

ENCOURAGEMENT

In order to preserve your deliverance, you must learn to encourage yourself to advance. Stop looking for people to encourage you. Everybody needs encouragement. Therefore, learn how to feed yourself instead of looking out for spoon-feeding and breast milking, for in the process of seeking breast milk, you may faint.

Although David was facing persecution and a death threat from King Saul, trusting that the purpose of God would be manifested some day, he encouraged himself to arise and possess the land of Israel. David fought and conquered the small villages around Israel on his own initiative. He used the Word of God to counsel himself, and to overcome strange interferences. By the time Saul died, David had subdued all the land and done away with most of Israel's enemies. Therefore:

- Learn to counsel yourself in the light of the Word of God.
- Learn to examine your decisions from a Biblical point of view as though you are advising or helping someone else (especially your child).
- Learn to discipline yourself as unto a child.
- Learn to teach and educate yourself and also make yourself available to be taught and to teach others.
- Learn to correct yourself and be subject to correction by others.
- Learn to submit yourself as you want and wish others to do to you.
- Learn to listen to yourself and to another, as expected from others.

PRAYER

I shall learn to discipline myself.
I shall learn to…*(fill in the words applicable to your need)*

DECISIONS

There are things you must decide never to do, if you want others to appreciate your deliverance and success. Cain could not teach himself the precepts of God, or counsel himself against the deception of the enemy, so he inherited the sin of his parents (Adam and Eve). Although he heard the warnings of God to desist from the evil decision he had at heart, pride did not allow him to resist the enemy. After committing the sin of murder, he also refused to repent. So he became a vagabond. Therefore examine your decisions in the light of His Word, and counsel yourself. Therefore:

- Never expect too much from another.
- Never victimize anyone
- Never listen to gossip
- Never find fault with another
- Never under-estimate another
- Never accuse another falsely
- Never depend on hearsay (I suspect people are thinking or saying...)
- Never humiliate another
- Never disgrace another
- Never interfere with another

PRAYER

I shall never listen to gossip.
I shall never...*(renounce the negative things in your life)*.

DETERMINATION

Determination is the foundation stone for deliverance. It is the solution to your maintenance. Despite the death of her husband, Ruth determined to cleave to her mother-in-law, Naomi. She was determined to serve the Lord God with Naomi at all cost. Her decision and determination paid off, as she won the favor of the whole nation of Israel, and became the grandmother of King David.

David inherited the motivation of pleasing God from her. That was a positive inheritance. Ruth was a woman who counseled herself and examined her decisions in the light of the Word. She stood against all odds to encourage herself, even before Naomi picked it up. So Ruth first built a strong foundation of encouragement into her own spirit and soul, then Naomi decided to support her decisions and determinations.

Ruth's character affected her mother-in-law and many others who watched her life. She was a woman who watched her ways. Therefore:

- Determine to hold on to the various decisions you have just taken as indicated above.
- Determine to walk out of physical captivity.
- Watch and correct your personal character.
- Watch and correct your human relations.
- Watch and correct your tolerance.
- Watch and correct your sensitivity *(Are you sensitive to the Holy Spirit or to the flesh?)*
- Watch and correct your behavior.
- Watch and correct your language.
- Watch and correct your approach toward others.
- Watch and correct your impressions.
- Watch and correct your perceptions.
- Watch and correct your imagination.
- Watch and correct your motives.
- Watch and correct your attitude.

PRAYER

I shall watch and correct my behavior.

I shall watch and correct...*(speak out the words applicable to you).*

Spiritual Captivity: Determine to break that covenant.

- Renounce, resist and stop the association
- Renounce, resist and stop the contribution
- Renounce, resist and stop the attendance
- Renounce, resist and stop the visitation

- Renounce, resist and stop the participation (willingly or unwillingly)
- Renounce, resist and stop the entertainment
- Renounce, resist and stop the fear
- Renounce, resist and stop the desire
- Renounce, resist and stop the communication
- Renounce, resist and stop the compromise

PRAYER

I shall renounce, resist and stop every negative interruption in my life.

I shall renounce, resist and stop ... *(renounce the negative behavior in your life)*.

Material Captivity: Determine to control your purchasing power.

- Rebuke and avoid ordinary wants
- Rebuke and avoid fashion vogue
- Rebuke and avoid covetousness
- Rebuke and avoid wastage
- Rebuke and avoid lust of material acquisition
- Rebuke and avoid the spirit of debt
- Rebuke and avoid lust of the eyes.
- Rebuke and avoid the spirit of buying unnecessarily.

Motivate your Determination

- Determine to guard against the various sins you have rebuked and renounced.
- Determine not to go over and lick your past vomit. The stench will destroy you

- Determine to preserve your friendship with the Lord Jesus Christ.
- Determine to cleave to your deliverance.

DECISION

Beloved, you have read through this book. You have been convicted in one way or another. Do not be angry with me.

This is not meant to hurt you, but to help correct your ways.
It will be a great joy in heaven if you can receive the conviction with honesty.

Go back to the portion(s) that convicted you and repent. Ask God to forgive and cleanse you with the blood of Jesus Christ.

As you do this, the peace of God will rest upon you and your life will never be the same again.
You will begin to hear the voice of God clearly and your utterances will be purified

As you study the Scriptures, you will receive power. Gradually, your utterances will gain effectiveness. The more you spend time with the Scriptures, the more you will be strengthened.

Out of the abundance of your heart you will gain from that which you have invested.

Watch what you do. Be very observant.
Be careful so that you do not reverse the Word of God.
Be careful so that you do not reject His pruning.

Your attitude can never change the Word of God.
What you think and expect cannot affect the Lord.
Be submissive, take in the truth and you will be blessed.

Pauline Walley Bible Training Center (PWBTC)

The Pauline Walley Bible Training Center is an institution for training leaders, individuals and church groups. It is an intensive practical training center where people are taught to build their image and personality, improve their ministry skills and abilities, develop their talents and gifts, minister to self, family members, friends and to church or fellowship members. In the process of training, people are also taught to be equipped for ministration and to face the battle of life as it is in the ministry.

The areas of study are:

School of Deliverance (SOD)
School of Strategic Prayer (SSP)
School of Tactical Evangelism (STE)
School of Mentoring and Leadership (SML)
School of the Gifts of the Holy Spirit (SGHS)
School of the Prophets (SOP)
School of Pulpit Communications (SPC)

The Pauline Walley Bible Training Center programs are organized and held in different parts of the world at various times. At seminar levels, one week or two weeks of intensive training are organized to help leaders and ministers or church/fellowship groups to establish various arms of Church ministry and also equip their members for such purposes.

Intensive training and a one-year certificate course are readily available in Bronx, New York and other regions, based on request. If you are interested in hosting any of these programs in your region or country or church/ministry, please contact us. See details of our contact and website on the back page.

Christian Books
by
DR. PAULINE WALLEY

THE AUTHORITY OF AN OVERCOMER: YOU CAN HAVE IT...I HAVE IT

The Authority of An Overcomer shares the real-life testimony of a day-to-day experience with the Lord Jesus Christ. It encourages you to apply the Word of God to every facet of your life, such as sleeping and waking with Jesus, walking and talking with Jesus, and dining with Him as you would with your spouse or a friend.

SOMEBODY CARES...CARES FOR YOU...CARES FOR ME

Somebody Cares...Cares for you...Cares for Me talks about the care that the Lord Almighty has for every one of us. It teaches you to care for other people and exercise tolerance toward their shortcomings. You will learn the importance of love and the true meaning as you read this book

RECEIVE AND MAINTAIN YOUR DELIVERANCE ON LEGAL GROUNDS.

Many people go from one prayer house to another, from the general practitioner to the specialist, from one minister to the Pope; and from one chapel to another church, with the same mission, aiming for the same expectation, yet never hitting the target. Why? Many people lack the knowledge of maintaining their healing and deliverance. This book, *Receive and Maintain Your Deliverance On Legal Grounds* will teach you to understand how to maintain what you receive from God.

ANGER: GET RID OF IT...YOU CAN OVERCOME IT

Anger is one of the many problems that people seek to resolve but lack the solution. Many have resigned their fate to it, thinking that it is a natural phenomenon. This book teaches about the causes of anger, and how to uproot them in order to receive your healing.

THE POWER OF THE SPOKEN WORD

There is a purpose for which we speak and when we speak; we expect something to happen in order for the purpose of the utterance to be fulfilled. This book teaches you to exercise your authority so that the word you speak will be manifested effectively.

THE HOLY SPIRIT: THE UNIQUENESS OF HIS PRESENCE.

The presence of the Holy Spirit highlights the difference between the gifts of the Spirit, the presence of God and the visitation of the Holy Spirit. In this book, you will learn to enjoy the delightful presence of the Holy Spirit in your spiritual walk.

THE HOLY SPIRIT: MAINTAIN HIS PRESENCE IN TRIALS AND TEMPTATIONS

This book teaches you how to maintain the presence of God, especially in trials and temptations. Oftentimes, when Christians go through difficult situations, they think they are alone. But that need not be. You can enter the presence of the Holy Spirit in difficult times and witness His Power to strengthen you and turn your situations around.

PROGRESSIVE ACHIEVEMENT: RECEIVE IT; MAINTAIN IT

This book teaches you how to move on continuously and overcome obstacles that usually frustrate prosperity. It enlightens you about the various types of progress that may come your way and how to manage them. It also encourages you to overcome failure and disappointment. The book also helps you to understand the concept of continuity and progressiveness as part of the characteristics of the Holy Spirit.

THE HOLY SPIRIT: POWER OF THE TONGUE

In recent times, many people have been seeking instant power and prophetic manifestations. Christians and ministers are indulging in all sorts of practices to demonstrate some special abilities to attract public attention. This book, *Power of the Tongue*, discusses the various powers and anointing(s) at work. It will help you to decipher between the Holy Spirit power and satanic powers. It will also teach you about the various anointing(s) that exist and how you can reach out for the genuine one.

PULLING DOWN SATANIC STRONGHOLDS: WAR AGAINST EVIL SPIRITS

Many Christians are under satanic attacks and influences, but very few people understand what the actual problems are. Some believe in God, but have no idea that there is anything like the satanic realm, yet they are under satanic torments. This book, *Pulling Down Satanic Strongholds*, enlightens you on some of the operations of the devil. It will help you know when an activity being performed around you is of the devil. This knowledge will strengthen you in prayer and equip you against the wiles of the enemy.

WHEN SATAN WENT TO CHURCH?

Many people fear the devil more than they fear God. At the mention of Satan or demons, they are threatened to death. Yet they are complacent in their own ways and yield to sin easily. Let the fear of God grip you and not the fear of Satan. This book enlightens you on the activities of the enemy within and around the church, the home and the Christian community. It helps you to identify battles and to put on your armor of warfare against the enemy. It also encourages you to hold firm the shield of faith. May the Lord enlighten your eyes of understanding as you read this book.

SOLUTION: DELIVERANCE MINISTRATION TO SELF AND OTHERS

Since the death of Jesus Christ on the cross, humans have been given the opportunity to experience and encounter the joy of salvation. However, lack of knowledge has kept the world in the dark and deprived them of the importance of Christianity. This book, *Solution: Deliverance Ministration to Self and Others* portrays just what the title says. It teaches you to understand the intricacies of deliverance ministration and to avoid the dangerous practices that have discouraged others. Read it and you will be blessed as never before.

Subscription

GOSPEL SONGS ON CASSETTE
Overcomers' Expression
Send Your Power
Vessels of Worship
Poetic Expression

BOOKS
All the books listed can be ordered

CONTACTS For Ministration:

WEST AFRICA
Pauline Walley School of Deliverance
P.O. Box MS 301, Mile-Seven, Accra, Ghana.
Tel/Fax: (233) 400907, 403063 or 404184

UNITED KINGDOM
Pauline Walley Christian Communications
P.O. Box 4673, London SE1 4UQ.
Tel: (44) 207-771-0053

UNITED STATES
Pauline Walley Christian Communications
P. O. Box 250, Bronx, NY 10467
Telephone (718) 652-2916/Fax (718) 405-2035
Email: paulinewalley@school-of-deliverance.com
paulinewalley@optonline.net
Website: www.paulinewalley.org
www.school-of-deliverance.com
www.overcomershouse.com

ABOUT THE BOOK

Receive and Maintain Your Deliverance talks about how a Christian can stay in the deliverance procured through Jesus Christ. Knowledge about the nature of deliverance is, however, paramount to its maintenance. The author cancels the myth that deliverance is banished to the ancient world; instead she examines the various deliverances recorded in Scriptures and couples them with her own experience in ministering deliverance to the oppressed all over the world. "Deliverance is as needed as ever before," she asserts. This book is a must for anyone struggling with deliverance in his or her life. It will change your life or the life of someone around you.

ABOUT THE AUTHOR

Pauline Walley is an ordained Prophet-Evangelist who teaches the **Word of God** with dramatic demonstrations. She is anointed by the Holy Spirit to teach the gospel of healing and deliverance, and to impart the message of love and joy to the people.

Pauline travels to various parts of the world, ministering in churches, crusades, revivals and seminars in a variety of academic institutions, as well as speaking to professional bodies. She is also talented in writing, drama, poetry and composing songs. Some of her musical works are also on record. She is also the author of ten other books (see inside back page for details on her books).

Pauline is the President of Pauline Walley Evangelistic Ministries and Christian Communications (PWEMCC), as well as the founder of the School of Deliverance (SOD) in New York, USA. The School trains ministers, groups and individuals all over the world. Before her call into full-time ministry, Pauline Walley, who holds a Masters degree in Journalism, was one of the few women in Sports Journalism. Pauline has completed her PhD in Pulpit Communications and Expository Preaching.

Published by Pauline Walley Christian Communications.
P.O. Box 4673, London, SE1 4UQ, UK (or)
P.O. Box 250, Bronx New York NY 10467, USA.

Printed in the United States
45925LVS00009B/58-81